Our Naughty Fat Cells

A Humorous Adult Tale with a Twist!
It's Told by Fat Cells!

Our Naughty Fat Cells

A Humorous Adult Tale with a Twist!
It's Told by Fat Cells!

Written and Illustrated by

Alice Hutchison

This book is dedicated with love to my wonderful husband Alan and my wonderful son Luke. Thank you both for your assistance and inspiration!

Contents

Introduction

I am the owner of a rich and varied collection of naughty fat cells. My fat cells have a tendency to pop-up wherever they want. They even have the audacity to congregate in areas of my body where I have posted signs: "**No Fat Cells Allowed**!" In fact, they dance upon my buttocks so often, my tape measure refuses to wrap itself around my ample ass!

After slicing the tape measure to ribbons, I felt a sense of empowerment. I had a talk with my fat cells, including the cellulite cells, which cling tenaciously to my thighs and buttocks. I decided my blubber blight would not be my undoing! In order to avoid insanity, I granted my fat cells my acceptance.

I could see the hand writing on the wall and it penned the word: Disgruntlement! I think not! I know a truce with my fat cells will encourage my stability. It is the perfect rationale.

Since I am a quasi-crazy person anyway, I plunged head first into concocting ways to defend human fat cells. After hours of mind-wrenching research, I learned adipose is another word for fat cell. With my new found knowledge, I triumphantly anointed myself an Adipose Advocate and a *Fatologist*! I state unequivocally and without reservation: "Humans cannot live without their fat cells!"

In fact, I was able to type this book thanks to the fat pads in my fingertips. Without them, it would have been skin and bones hitting the keys. Ouch! Fat cells act as connective tissue, energy reserves and organ insulators among other things. They help humans maintain, *homeostasis*; which means the body is functioning normally.

I know there are two sides to every story. History shows the constant struggles humans had as they tried to maintain their health. I applaud everyone who tries to improve the lives of humans. Millions of humans struggle with weight issues.

It does not mean they are unhealthy individuals. Healthy and fit humans come in all sizes. No one deserves to be bullied because they carry extra weight upon their frame.

Please remember, fat cells did not ask to be born. Many humans have mistaken beliefs about them. I wrote this book from the perspective of fat cells because I think they deserve our understanding, and because they bugged the hell out of me to have their say! They were very persistent! To get them off my back (because I knew they were reluctant to leave my ass), I agreed to let them tell their stories. In order to amass data for this book, I encouraged the fat cells to traverse the *fatosphere* for information. In the interest of fair play, both female and male fat cells were given free rein. They used poetic license to tell their fat facts, cellulite conundrums and pudgy puzzles.

I provided pertinent data about fat cells and cellulite cells at the beginning of the book. For the purpose of clarity, adipose cells are always referred to as fat cells in this book.

The fat cells' stories start in the section titled: "Human Personalities/*Personutilties*."

This book was written so everyone will have a better understanding of their fat cells. Bon *fat-appétit*!

The Dawn of Humans

The dawn of humankind was cold and bleak. Due to fluctuating amounts of food, humans were finding it hard to make their way.

God looked down from Heaven and said, "No one is laughing! What's wrong now? It looks like I have a new problem. This is bad timing! I was really looking forward to getting a back rub from the new angel! Now I have to postpone it! Darn it! The sooner I get this problem solved, the better. Humans! You can't live with them, and you can't live without them! I guess it's time the poor puny humans have some fun and laughter. They will need stronger bodies before the festivities can begin. I'm going to put some meat on their bones. I will create *fat cells*. They will perk up the humans' appetites causing them to eat more. Once the humans have gained weight and strength, they will feel like laughing. The sounds of their laughter will rise up to Heaven and finally give me peace of mind. Thank God. . . oh… that's me!"

With the passage of time, many humans gained weight. Laughter could be heard echoing throughout the hills and valleys.

As the tide of humanity swelled, an evil wind blew across the land; with it came famine, pestilence and death. Many humans suffered from malnutrition. Mobs of angry humans with clubs tormented one another. Most humans died out. No one laughed anymore.

God looked down from the soft pink cloud he rode upon and became angry. "What the heck is going on down there? I don't hear any laughter!" he thundered. The roar of his words swirled the oceans and ripped trees from their earthen footings.

The humans sensed immediate danger, and their fear caused them to taunt one another with maniacal glee.

"Shut up you fools! My will shall prevail. For my sanity's sake I have to prove to myself that I haven't failed with my project called… *Laughter*! Pay attention! I hereby decree: 'Fat cells shall be more potent. They will provide energy, strength and laughter for humans so humankind can survive forever!'" shouted God.

"What the hell are fat cells?" shouted the humans.

"Do I have to explain everything to you creatures? You shall have taste buds placed upon your tongues!" bellowed God.

"What the hell are taste buds?" screamed the humans as they cringed in fear.

"Morons! They help you taste your food. Eat more food!" shouted God.

As the years went by the humans obeyed God's word and increased their food consumption. During thousands of years of human development fat cells increased in number. They became an integral part of human anatomy. Fat cells encouraged growth and helped maintain the physical integrity of the human body.

Humans became more fun loving and extended good will toward one another. They shared jokes and laughter. Humans of all shapes and sizes were born thus giving rise to an infinite number of fat cells.

Fat Cell Exposure

Fat cells are. . . everywhere! Just like bunnies they multiply rapidly! As soon as humans turn their backs, fat cells spring into action. Before they know it, humans have pudginess which refuses to budge! Fat cells call this, *fat facilitation.*

How do fat cells do this? First off, they ain't no dummies; they're practically geniuses! Fat cells have a crafty brain called the *nucleus* in their lipid filled pudgy bodies. The nucleus works in tandem with the *mitochondria* which are the powerhouses of fat cells. These cellular components have a unique ability to gauge humans' physical and emotional hunger needs. When humans say they are hungry, fat cell ears perk up.

"What's that? You want something to eat? Go ahead, go ahead! Eat! Eat! Eeeeeeeeeat!" say the fat cells.

Yes, it is true! Fat cells are ready for humans to eat anything, anytime, anywhere. Fat cells want humans to fall under their spell. If humans succumb, they are enveloped in a fog of fatness. Fat cells are always on the alert ready to puff up like balloons when humans eat too much. That is how pudginess occurs!

Fat cells have an agenda which demands their proliferation. They have a tenacious desire to live life to the fullest. Not only do fat cells want their pudgy bodies to swell, they want their population to explode as well.

Fat cells are hardworking! They carry out tremendous tasks in humans. The jobs performed by fat cells are not easy. Keep in mind their fat cell brains are egging them on by shouting, "Swell up, swell up! Do your jobs. . . damn it! You're not in humans just to look pretty!

The poor fat cells are being prompted by both sides. Their bossy brains are insisting they retain their fullness while the humans are whining they want to be thinner. What are fat cells to do? They probably would like to have a stiff drink but that is out of the question. Instead they do what fat cells do best. They throw back their shoulders and belt out a chorus of their favorite songs: "We've got to be fat," or "We'll do it our way!"

After the fat cells are rejuvenated by their singing, they go back to dutifully serving humans. It's in their DNA to be that way. Fat cells know they are ordained to give humans energy, strength and laughter.

Humans should never underestimate fat cells. They are pudgy potent powerhouses! Fat cells know humans cannot live without them. Humans know the truth of the matter. They are in an endless dance of give and take with their fat cells. Whether the dance is a waltz or a tango, fat cells just want a little respect and a lot of laughter from humans!

Fatpocrates:
The Champion of Fat Cells

The nucleus of the fat cell, also referred to as the blubber brain, reigns supreme in the annals of nuclei history. These nuclei earned their supremacy by helping to ensure the proper placement of fat cells in the human body. They did so with the help of a brilliant fat cell named Fatpocrates. He was held in high esteem and considered by many to be the Father of Fat Medicine.

Fatpocrates put his superior intellect to good use by furthering the co-dependency between fat cells and humans. He knew fat cells would have to be stored until they were called for service in different parts of the humans. Thanks to him fat cell depots were created to house immature and recycled fat cells.

Fatpocrates knew the humans' internal organs were vital for survival. Thanks to his advice, millions of fat cells were plastered like shiny mosaics against the organs. He knew they would insulate and protect the organs and insure humankinds' health and longevity. Fatpocrates and the fat cells secured a bond with humans guaranteed to last through all of eternity. All fat cells celebrated.

Unfortunately, the celebration was interrupted by a group of renegade nerve cells who escaped from the brain. They detested fat cells and called them useless blobs of blubber.

Fatpocrates became alarmed and shouted, "Attention nerve cells, end this insanity! My fellow fat cells have successfully located themselves throughout the entire human body.
They have even provided protective sheaths around your nerve cells. My advice to you is return to the human brain. The humans will need millions of nerve cells. They will need help with their thought processes because someday politicians will try to lead them around like sheep. Nerve cells can help

humans to think for themselves, and fat cells can help them to laugh."

The nerve cells realized Fatpocrates was right and returned to the brain. Sadly, thousands of them suffered through months of inactivity as they waited patiently to be used in the thinking process. Some of them filled hope chests full of tidbits of knowledge as they waited to provide answers to unspoken questions.

Fat cells on the other hand were vigorously defending their positions and renewing their population. With their skill and cunning adaptability, they continued to make fat cell history.

Fatistotle:
The Advent of Cellulite Cells

As humans gained weight and physical strength some of their fat cells were affected by hormones. A lot of fat cells were transformed into a variety called cellulite. The cellulite cells looked slightly different. Most of them were viewed as intruders. Tension increased between the two groups because many fat cells were relegated to lesser roles. Thousands of them were forced to provide foundation for cellulite cells. Most cellulite cells expressed appreciation for the structural support. However, some of these cells flaunted their positions and bragged they were the most important fat cells in humans.

Their uppity behavior caused some fat cells to consider anarchy. This threat caused panic among the non-rebellious fat cells. They decided to institute a form of severe punishment for those fat cells who endangered their humans. With that in mind, the Feces Flow Dipping Vat was created as a deterrent for any fat cells who were stupid enough to misbehave!

Fatistotle, the brilliant thinker known for his wise logic, was summoned to give advice and discourage the possibility of anarchy. He was escorted to the meeting by a contingency of fat cell guards. Several of Fatistotle's devoted students trailed meekly behind him. Fatistotle pondered the issue for two days and nights. His students gazed adoringly at him while they awaited his decision. When Fatistotle stood up, several fat cells became animated. They beckoned to one another to remain quiet so all fat cells could hear his speech.

"Attention all fat cells and cellulite cells of the human body. Ours is a dilemma not easily solved. My logic tells me, it was our destiny to be born as fat cells. However, my ethics tell me to question the validity of one's permanent station in life. Shouldn't all fat cells be considered equal? The only true and just solution to this problem shall be a series of rotational duties in which most fat cells spend time in the cellulite cells' locations," said Fatistotle.

"No!" screamed a furious fat cell! "I am from a distinguished line of ancestral breast fat cells who fill the female breasts. It is my heritage. I will not undo the accomplishments of my ancestors!"

"She's right, we are what we are! I'm ass fat, and ass fat I'll always be!" shouted a bloated buttocks fat cell as he belched forth a bit of stinky air.

"Back off you bellowing beast of ass fat," commanded the leader of the fat cell guards. "I am in charge here. We will give Fatistotle the admiration and respect he deserves. While you have been moaning and groaning about your fate, my fellow fat cell guards have been securing the periphery of this room. Line up all of you! You will do what Fatistotle says. If there are any among you who refuse to share in the cellulite cells' duties, you will be taken to the Feces Flow Dipping Vat and repeatedly dunked!"

"Just a moment! I will institute fair play into my program. You will have a cellulite cell curriculum to enhance the education of fat cells. I think a cellulite cell charm school would be appropriate too. Please do as I ask. It is true that cellulite cells have a slightly altered appearance, but they are fat cells too. You must all work together. I am confident all of you will adapt to your additional responsibilities. Due to the nature of their duties, the brain, anal and rectal fat cells are exempt from my plan. All of the rest of you are subject to rotational duties. All fat cells can avoid the Feces Flow Dipping Vat if they heed my words. The leader of the fat cell guards will instruct you in your duties. I will take my leave now," said Fatistotle as he waved and left the building.

Thanks to Fatistotle's inspirational guidance, fat cells and cellulite cells worked together to build two learning centers for all fat cells. Inscribed on the buildings are: *Fatistotle Cellulite Cell Curriculum Center and Fatistotle Cellulite Cell Charm Center.* They became hives of activity where fat cells and cellulite cells shared their visions and ideas. As time went by, both types of fat cells elected a committee comprised of an equal number of fat cells and cellulite cells. This committee was in charge of creating educational materials for all fat cells.

Due to the physical and mental complexities of their roles in the human bodies, the committee took ideas directly from the human hosts. They believed it was only natural for them to combine anecdotal observations with their scientific findings. With that in mind, the committee created the lessons, rules and credos for all fat cells which are still in effect today.

The language used by humans is of particular interest to fat cells. In order to make themselves feel more at home, fat cells adopt all sorts of slang words from humans. When the mood grabs them, some fat cells even invent their own words.

The committee oversees the placement of both types of fat cells in different parts of the humans. The committee also coordinates the publication of educational materials. These publications are used to educate both types of fat cells.

The lessons and rules vary in size and scope. The lessons about human body parts are in their own section. They consist of pertinent information about the interactions between humans and fat cells. Additional lessons about fat cells and cellulite cells follow the human body parts. The credos are designed to be inspirational.

In all societies, there are individuals who misbehave. Among the fat cells there are fat felons, cellulite cell criminals and pudgy perpetrators. A medical facility called the Psycho/Sicko Center was built to house these deranged individuals. They receive medical and mental care from the famous psychiatrist Dr. R. U. Nuttee and his assistants.

What follows is the educational text written by the committee. The committee uses the word "we" for educational purposes.

Human Personalities/*Personutilties*

We wish to remind fat cells and cellulite cells, it is an honor and privilege to serve humans. At least that is what we keep telling ourselves over and over (maybe someday we will even believe it).

Human beings are unique creatures who come in all shapes, sizes and colors. And lots of them are nuts! Okay, there are many humans who are normal; however, we are not sure where they are hiding. When normal humans finally make an appearance, fat cells will do all they can to keep them from going nuts.

Humans have all kinds of personalities. The word should be *personutilties*. Humans even coined phrases which use the word nuts to describe one another. They say:

"He's nuts!"

"She's nutty!"

"What a nutcase!"

"He's a hard nut to crack!"

After thousands of years of watching human behavior, many of our fat cells were in fear of becoming nuts too. Nuts to that idea! We have a job to do. Educating fat cells about humans is a titanic task, so let's get started! Fat cells think God had an epiphany after he created male humans.

"What the heck have I done?" shouted God. After he threw out some thunderbolts and lightning, he calmed down and said, "Of course! The solution is obvious. I will create female humans!"

The creation of females worked splendidly for males. The two sexes paired up nicely which provided equal opportunities for everyone to go nuts! From what fat cells have seen, nuttiness runs rampant in many humans!

With this in mind, let us get down to the nitty-gritty about personutilties. Each human is born with something called an

EGO. It is like a human clock. Some of them are running a little slow, others are running fast, and the rest may need to be reset. Humans' egos involve them in all kinds of daily dramas. Fat cells believe EGO stands for <u>E</u>motional <u>G</u>esturing <u>O</u>mnivore. We know emotions run through humans with every breath they take.   Humans gesture when they eat, talk and perform tasks. Most humans are omnivores and eat different kinds of food. Fat cells believe these are the three components which explain the word EGO.

Thanks to their egos, humans have very complicated personutilties. Some humans become self absorbed and behave in an egotistical manner. They have delusions of grandeur which may cause egomania. These humans may be labeled egomaniacs. Watch out for these types of humans! Many of them push themselves to the limits of their physical endurance. Fat cells may have to work overtime to provide extra energy for egomaniacs. Just be sure your little fat brains do not get carried away and turn you into *fatgomaniacs*!

Fat cells beware! Most humans believe they are in charge of their lives. Really! When? From what we can tell their hormones try to control them, and they crack a mean whip! When hormones snap their whips, nuttier actions may overtake humans.   Hormones are bossy!   They encourage moody behavior in humans which often causes confusion. As a result, a lot of humans are unable to think properly. Some of them act as though their brains are in limbo. Fat cells have dubbed this a *hormonal hex*!

Fortunately, there is a form of electronic stimulation which snaps humans out of the hormonal hex and puts them into *Laughter/Drama Land*. Laughter/Drama Land is a fantastic place where comedies, dramas and other scenarios are shown for humans' enjoyment. Humans accomplish this by watching an electronic machine called a *television*. This magical box also called the T.V. is a blessing for fat cells. This is a perfect scenario for all fat cells. It lets humans experience a variety of emotions without leaving their homes. They laugh, cry, laugh again and then eat. Yes! Yes! Yessssssssssssss! Eat! The fat cells are hungry too! Just think, humans are able to eat and laugh while watching an electronic machine. This has been amazing for fat cells to witness. It encompasses both goals they were ordained to fulfill in humans; survival and laughter!

As stated before, humans are very emotional. Some fat cells believe the nutty behavior found in humans leads to laughter. Interesting! It's a plausible possibility! Hmm! We have to revoke a previous statement. From now on, fat cells will no longer curtail humans who are going nuts. Let normal humans go nuts if they want. Go ahead and bring on the nuts and their laughter. It is good for all of us!

In this lesson, we stressed the influence of human hormones. We did this to let fat cells know what some humans go through. You will learn more about human personalities/personutilties and their various body parts as you continue to read the lessons, rules and credos.

Please remember this credo: "Be patient when located in humans who are nuts, after all. . . they're only human!"

The Human Brain/Mind

The human brain is a large organ filled with gray matter. Some fat cells think it is filled with crazy matter. Whether it is gray or crazy, what really matters is how humans use the matter when they formulate their thoughts.

From what fat cells can tell, the human brain is like a black hole in outer space. Some stuff goes in and never comes out! This is what happens to most fat cells in the brain. Thousands of them fill the protective sheaths that encase the nerve cell transmitters. Once fat cells are sheathed in the brain, we rarely see them again. It is imperative they hold their positions. Otherwise, the nerve cell transmissions would zip around like bolts of electricity from damaged power lines! Sparks could fly out from the human's ears and that would be scary!

Attention! We are aware of some roving fat cells who abandon their locations to snoop around in other areas. Be warned: "DO NOT TRAVEL TO THE EARS TO SEE SHOOTING SPARKS!" Fat cells who do this, will see more than sparks when they are punished in the Feces Flow Dipping Vat! We reiterate, the only fat cells allowed in the ears are the ones serving rotations there.

Fat cells in the brain are vital for normal thought processes; however, they do not create those thoughts. Fat cells just deliver them. Thank goodness for that! Fat cells have no desire to lay claim to some of the crazy ideas that come from humans! We have enough trouble keeping track of our own naughty fat cells who have lost their marbles! In fact we have more crazy fat cells than we know what to do with! However, we are more than happy to help deliver human thoughts. When their delivery system works properly, it is the best system on earth!

Before fat cells delve too deeply into the human brain, we must let them know an important fact. There are not enough words in anyone's lexicon to explain how the unusual organ called the brain works. Why is that? How the hell should we know? We are only fat cells! We're just going to wing it!

Get ready! It is time for fat cells to navigate the human brain. As you stand quivering on the precipice of the brain, go ahead and shake with fear! You are about to plunge into the chasm of the unknown. Try not to scream too loudly!

The inside of the human brain is filled with a mysterious entity called the *mind*. For hundreds of years, medical researchers and scientists have tried to figure out how the blasted thing works! And to this day, they are still trying! They gather together in groups and create *think tanks*. Fat cells believe the researchers or *thinker tinkers* desire to pick each others' brains. Just like *Fatdin's* famous sculpture "The Thinker" these great thinkers rack their brains to collect their thoughts. They want to *brainstorm*!

These scientists want to know what other humans have on their minds. They want to read the minds of their fellow thinkers. Fat cells wonder if this is a good idea. If someone is deep in thought and another human tries to delve into their thoughts, the resulting thoughts could create fractured thoughts which may make both parties appear thought-less. If a human's mind is full of thoughts, does that mean the human is thoughtful?

All this talk of thinking has made the fat cells hungry! Since we are discussing the human brain and thought processes, it is a good time to remind fat cells of the catchy phrase: "Food for thought!" What a marvelous quote! Fat cells everywhere applaud the genius who first spoke those three words. It makes many of us feel like doing back flips. Unfortunately, most fat cells are a little too pudgy for that!

When humans apply their minds in think tanks, they do need some food for thought. After all, they may have hungry fat cells in there. Great thinkers need great food! After they make up their minds to eat some nutritious foods, they can resume thinking. Speaking of making up their minds, some humans

23

seem unable to do so. They think of one thing, then another thing and then they forget what they were thinking about in the first place! At this point humans claim they have too much on their minds! Oh. . . never mind!

Fat cells have something else on their minds. Humans cling to and use the phrase: "Mind over matter!" This presents a pudge puzzle. As we scratch our fat heads to figure out this phrase, many of us feel we are in over our heads. From what we can tell, humans desire to separate the gray matter in their brains from their minds. Fat cells wonder why! Maybe they do not like the color gray. We suppose it is possible humans want to expand their minds and are looking for extra room. Even though it sounds like insanity to fat cells, it often results in bursts of creativity for humans. Lots of fun and crazy stuff happens! Many fat cells believe that is how *modern art* got its start.

Fat cells notice when humans' creative juices start to flow, their appetites increase as well. During this time, some humans direct their energy towards creating new recipes. Why not? Creativity wears many faces. It excites fat cells to know humans want to investigate different foods and different ways to prepare them. Trying new recipes is always fun. It is our job to insure humans eat enough to sustain themselves.

Humans attach significance to the phrase: "The mind has a mind of its own!" Oh no. . . now they have two minds! Doesn't that only happen with Gemini's? Talk about mind-boggling! Fat cells are not equipped to deal with two minds. How are we going to know who to send where? We are going to be stumbling over each other. Oh great, now we are flabbergasted flab! Not for long! Here's the deal, humans have only one mind... thank goodness! It is filled with thoughts and secrets. It should have been clear from the onset of scientific plundering of the brain, the elusive human mind is not ready to divulge its secrets... yet! So researchers, let your minds be at rest. Otherwise, you may lose your minds trying to figure out how human minds work!

Fat cells do not mean to act smug, but exploring the depths of human minds, makes us wonder if we are losing our minds! Is craziness contagious? Is insanity inevitable? Is lunacy looming? We hope not! Oh. . . forgive us! Fat cells know we should be mindful of our comments. We will try to keep that in our minds, as we continue to examine human minds.

Some fat cells in the brain made an interesting discovery. They believe human minds are similar to kaleidoscopes. These fat cells think the thoughts held by humans are like exquisite pieces of glass which twirl constantly in their minds. Most human thoughts, assisted by nerves and fat cells, become aligned in a proper manner. When this happens, humans behave in a productive and normal way. Whatever normal is? For you see, some humans choose to loosely define the word normal. In fact, many humans stretch the word normal to fit their particular idiosyncrasies, psychoses and phobias. If humans are crazier than loons, nuttier than fruitcakes or ditzier than dingbats, they may call themselves normal! At that point, none of the fat cells want to argue with those nutcases. When mining the minefields known as the human minds, fat cells need positive mindsets. With that in our minds, we accept a liberal interpretation of the word normal.

Fat cells are reluctant to pigeonhole any humans into prescribed manners of behavior; unless those manners pertain to eating! We believe there is one word which must twirl incessantly through human minds: **Food!** Some thoughts of food could be:

"I want to have a healthy salad today!"

"Forget the salad, I want a pizza!"

"I have a date with a platter full of fresh vegetables!"

"Remember, you promised to make my favorite cake!"

Those comments represent just a few of the thoughts which humans may have about food. Some fat cells think thoughts of food provoke feelings of comfort and happiness in humans. We are certain thoughts of food go back to the dawn of humankind. Fat cells believe if humans lost their ability to think of food, they would really go *bonkers*! Humans would run around like psyched out *crazoids* screaming:

"Something profound has slipped our minds!"

"We are missing thoughts that are key to our survival."

"It's a thought hidden deep within the recesses of our minds that starts with the letter, 'F!'"

Fortunately for humans and fat cells, humans will always have food on their minds!

In addition to fostering thoughts of food, human minds oversee the senses of sight, hearing, taste, smell and touch. Those senses are expertly controlled by human brains.

Fat cells believe there is one sense in which human brains surrender their control. It is the most intriguing sense of all, the *sense of humor.* It is the one sense that keeps fat cells infatuated with humans. We love their sense of humor. Most humans are funny. God was brilliant when he gave humans laughter! Amazingly, among the throngs of humans, there are some lucky ones who have a *heightened sense of humor.* Yesssssss! Make us laugh! Make us laugh! Fat cells think these humans have two kinds of appetites. One for food and one for laughter. Well, maybe a third too. . . a *fatpetite*!

Humans, who appreciate whimsy, use their minds to create fanciful things so their fellow humans can have fun! They make unique items such as: whoopee cushions, balloons, bumper stickers, party supplies and other delightful things! These humans love to laugh. They are a delight to be around and are truly appreciated by their fellow humans. Needless to say, fat cells love them too!

On the other end of the spectrum, there are humans that lack a sense of humor. They have been labeled by other humans as: sourpusses, pessimists, killjoys, malcontents, grumps, etc. Fat cells wonder where these humans left their laughter. It must be lost somewhere in the black holes of their minds. It is probably trapped in there, dying to get out! This bugs the hell out of fat cells! They want the laughter out and want it out now! This is not a laughing matter! It is one of the most serious situations which affects fat cells. As you know, we strive for laughter in humans. Most humans make this very easy for fat cells. However, sourpusses and grumps are usually ill-humored curmudgeons; they can undo many fat cell accomplishments. We want all of you to be on the alert for non-laughing humans. If fat cells are located in a human with a laughter deficiency, prepare yourselves for a lot of work. Institute a plan in which all fat cells work together; in other words, *dump the grumps*! Make them laugh!

We continue this lesson with information about humans who have extraordinary intellectual abilities. They are often referred to as *brainiacs*. These brainy individuals with the aid of fat cells help to perpetuate humankind. When brainiacs go into their *think tanks* to brainstorm, their brilliant ideas ricochet off the walls!

Thanks to their wonderful minds, brainiacs invent countless items which help other humans. We cannot forget the inventors of foodstuffs. Brainiacs with special knowledge of nutrition (also called nutritionists) help millions of humans to live healthy lives. They even invent food items for special occasions; some of which are sweets. Hmm! That is an important word in fat cells' language. Alright, we admit our little fat brains get excited at the thought of sweets! We cannot help it; some of us have a sweet tooth! For humans with a sweet tooth, fat cells hope they will eat sweets in moderation. No that doesn't sound right. We don't want humans to eat sweets in moderation. Fat cells want humans to go crazy with sweets! Crazy! Crazy! Crazy!

We better retract the previous statement or they may take us to the Feces Flow Dipping Vat! We are sorry, fat cells don't want humans to go crazy with sweets. We want humans to eat sweets in moderation and eat nutritious foods as well.

We wish we could end this lesson on a positive note. We cannot! It is our duty to provide all fat cells with a well rounded education about humans. You must realize humans undergo physical and mental stresses every day of their lives. Sometimes their normal thoughts become fragmented, and some humans appear to have lost their minds. We wish we could help the humans find them but there is a limit to what fat cells can do. For all we know the missing human minds could be in outer space or in the clutches of aliens. Oh no! Now it sounds as though we are losing our minds! Look... the best thing for fat cells to do is prepare themselves to witness utter madness in some humans. Hopefully, the impaired humans will seek help from medical professionals. The professionals will either help to make them better or screw them up even more! Either way it is out of the fat cells' little pudgy hands. However, if you are overly concerned, humans may squeak out a laugh or two when you tug on their funny bones. Give it a try! Humor can take their minds off their minds while they are waiting for the loose screw in their minds to be screwed back down.

Fat cells have compiled the following anecdotal phrases humans say about losing their minds:

"She may go off her rocker!"

"He could fly off the handle!"

"She came unglued at the seams!"

In case fat cells get any crazy ideas of their own, do not attempt to flee if your humans come unglued! Remember, one of your jobs is to serve as connective tissue. Fat cells are not under the human skin just for the fun of it! So keep your pudgy, fat bodies ready to re-glue your humans! At this point, they will need their fat cells more than ever. Your time in the humans cannot always be a barrel of laughs. All fat cells must remember, humans are complex beings who have a lot on their minds. Be ready! The humans will need your help if they crack up and lose their minds!

Here is a credo for fat cells: "Respect the fat cells in the brain, they are subject to stress and strain!"

The Human Face

The human face is one of the most beautiful creations fat cells will ever see. We feel our presence in the face is a triumph for all of us. Our location inside the mouth, within the facial cheeks, enables fat cells to help humans in two ways. We encourage humans to eat and to laugh. Wow... talk about a big job! Who's important now? The fat cells are, that's who! We get to work in the ingenious structure called the human mouth.

"Wait just a minute! Some fat cells refuse to believe this. It sounds too good to be true. Isn't it dark and wet in the mouth? What are fat cells getting themselves into? You can't fool us! Fat cells know the mouth is a big hole filled with teeth that could take a bite out of us! We have seen human teeth, and we want no part of those *choppers*! In addition, fat cells will be smashed up against the cheeks as all kinds of food slides by. We will barely be able to breathe! And if our human drinks alcohol, fat cells run the risk of becoming pickled pudge. We refuse to go into the human mouth!"

Attention fat cells! The comments contained in the previous paragraph were included to educate you about the dangers of rebellious behavior. Outbursts from insane fat cell anarchists will not be tolerated! We are not monsters who desire to catch fat cells every time they make a mistake. Well... okay we are! But... and it's a big but! There is a reason for our vigilance. The reason is: "God ordained fat cells to serve humans!" Get this through you thick fat cell heads! We demand obedience from all of you. If any fat cells fail to comply, they will be escorted to the Feces Flow Dipping Vat for their punishment.

As we were saying before the anarchists' outbursts, human mouths are ingenious structures. Talk about busy places! If humans are not talking, they are eating. Their mouths are incredible! Not only can humans use their mouths to eat, but the wonderful sound called laughter comes from there as well. Humans' laughter is spontaneous and amazing. It requires no

29

thought; it just comes out. Laughter is one of the best things that can happen to humans. Fat cells love the melodious sound of laughter because it means humans are happy, and when they are happy, they smile and eat! Yea! Great news for fat cells! How else are they going to keep their plump, shapely figures?

If fat cells were to poll humans about their favorite experiences, most of them would remember delicious meals and happy moments filled with laughter. Food and laughter help humans feel safe and comfortable.

Once fat cells are in the face, they will understand how vital food is to humans. Thanks to their taste buds, most humans enjoy eating. Taste buds are special receptors on human tongues which enable them to detect flavors. Taste buds are fat cells' *best buds* in all ways and always! When humans eat, their taste buds come alive. Fat cells will be amazed at all the delicious foods humans consume. They may even get to laugh at the faces their humans make when tasting sour and bitter foods.

Fat cells call humans who know a great deal about food, *Foodologists*; however, these humans call themselves *Foodies.* There are millions of them. Yesssss! Foodies are fat cells favorite humans! They know the intrinsic value of food and love sharing it with each other.

Attention fat cells, prepare yourselves for a startling fact! There are humans who think eating is a waste of time.

"WHAT? NO! THAT CANNOT BE TRUE! REALLY?"

"Where the hell did those humans come from?"

"Send them back! They cannot be normal!"

"They sound like unfriendly *Nonfoodies* to us!"

"What planet are they from? It has be out of our solar system! We do not want a bunch of fat hating aliens running around!"

"Fat cells have enough to do dealing with regular humans who inhabit the Earth!"

"No, no, there is no way any Nonfoodie aliens could have come through the Earth's radiation belt…we hope!"

"Silence you paranoid pudge balls, there are no aliens!"

"Pull your plump selves together so we can continue to educate you. Please refrain from further outbursts!"

As previously stated, some humans have little interest in what they eat. Fat cells believe these humans may have taste buds that malfunction which causes them to lose their interest in food. These humans may eventually turn into Nonfoodies. These are dire situations and must be dealt with quickly. Fat cells must not freak out! Do not attempt to run for your lives. Fat cells are not going to get off that easy! All fat cells which are in the tongues must tickle the taste buds. Hopefully, this stimulation will help humans enjoy their food and convert them back into Foodies.

We must expose fat cells to a grim reality. Some humans engage in a nasty trend called a *DIET*. What an awful word! Drop the *T* and you have the word *DIE*! Doesn't that just say it all! None of the fat cells want to die!

Humans on diets are called *dieters*. Watch Out! They are out to get you! At some point in the human's life, a critical event occurred. Perhaps, it was when a prom dress was deemed too tight or when a male was chided for fat spillage hanging over his belt. It might have been when a small child called another human a blimp. Whatever it was, it caused them to start a diet. Humans on diets can be like wild animals, you never know which way they will turn. They may not even know themselves. It is hard for them to keep track of things when their minds are churning with thoughts of food. Food, food it plagues them so!

Dieters may be the types of individuals who think eating all kinds of raw vegetables will help them lose weight. Yeah, maybe so, but at what cost? The loss of their minds! Fat cells believe some strange tasting vegetables are not even worth the time it takes to chew them. We are talking about rutabagas, turnips, kohlrabi, okra and radishes. Even their names sound bad! If there was a vegetable hell, they would all be there!

Do not let the radish's pretty, red disguise fool you. Woe to the fabulous color red to have been used in this manner. Obviously, the great Vegetable God took pity upon the radish and cloaked it in red so humans would use it as a garnish. He knew no one would eat it otherwise. Anyway, none of those nasty vegetables have any discernible fat and that our fellow fat cells explains why they taste yucky!

Dieters become obsessed with fat! They attempt to remove as much of it as possible from their diets. Their diets may become unbalanced. This will place fat cells in precarious positions. All of you must hold fast, and let your mitochondria lead the way. Use all of your strength to keep yourselves plump. With any luck, the dieters will eat something besides those cold crummy vegetables. Most humans do not stay on wacky diets very long. After a couple of weeks, they will say:

"The hell with this rabbit food!"

"We want some real food!"

At this point, you may see the dieters eat like they have never eaten before. They may begin a period of gorging. Some additional fat cells may come into your area. Please remember to accommodate the newcomers in a nice way.

Attention all fat cells! The mouth and lips are used for more than food consumption. Leave it to humans to figure out there is something else they can do with their lips. Namely, pucker up, smooch and kiss! Yes, yes! Kissing is special, kissing is romantic and kissing is fun. So what! So is eating!

Yes, we are aware of the statement by our famous fat cell writer, von Fatoethe, "A sweet smooch is similar to the right reply!"

In this instance, fat cells believe the *right reply* should be: "After an appropriate amount of kisses, humans should put their lips to forks and spoons and dine the night away!"

A credo for facial fat cells: "Fat cells will display grace, while in the human's face!"

The Human Eyes

Someone once said: "The eyes are the windows to the soul!" Maybe so, but when fat cells peek in there, they only see a couple of colored orbs. Not really, we are only kidding! The eyes are so much more than orbs! The eyes are magicians who enable humans to see all sorts of wondrous sights. In the twinkling of an eye humans make judgments based upon what they have seen. That is when it gets tricky! Some humans are not sure what they have seen. Many of them think their eyes are playing tricks on them. For you see, some humans may have spent too much time in *Laughter/Drama Land*. It might be wise to rest their eyes and take a vacation from there!

Fat cells feel humans should be open to all sorts of educational diversions. We want them *to see the light.* Which light? Well, the one in the refrigerator for starters! Humans may need a bite of food before they start their next endeavor.

Fat cells believe reading is a wonderful diversion. When we see humans read, it is a *sight for sore e*yes, especially if those humans are reading cookbooks! You know what that means. It is time for humans to cook and eat! Yum! Let's gorge! Oh forgive us; we got carried away! Fat cells don't really want humans to eat everything in sight! We just want them to eat good food that keeps them healthy. Good food makes for good eyesight. Good eyesight enhances reading. . . and eating!

There is another reason fat cells love reading. It creates laughter. Humans laugh when they read the comic strips in the newspapers. The comic strips, also called *the funnies*, are created by brilliant cartoonists who want their fellow humans to have laughter and fun. Isn't it remarkable there are geniuses among humankind who are perfectly tuned into the notion that humans need laughter. It's as if those perceptive individuals were created to help fat cells. Fat cells give special thanks to the writers of comics, jokes and other funny stories!

Please be advised only a select number of elite fat cells will serve time in the eyes. The rotations occur deep in the eye sockets, below the eyes near the cheek bones and along the brow bones. Generally speaking, these are spectacular locations to serve rotations. The fat cells will see many marvelous sights there, and they should be proud to serve humans in their *baby blues, browns* or *greens*. However, there will be times when fat cells should avert their eyes. Do not spy on humans who are engaged in. . . sexual activities! Do not be a peeping Tom! Keep your naughty fat cell eyes closed!

We must address a unique physical characteristic of the eyes. It is a liquid called tears. Humans have fountains in their eyes which flow forth when they cry. Fat cells don't know where all the water comes from! It gets wet. Really wet! Humans start crying when they are babies and never stop! By the time they are adults, humans have honed crying into a fine art. Crying is also known as *shedding tears*!

Crying is the opposite of laughing! When humans cry, salty water flows out from the tear ducts which are located in the corners of their eyes. Tears are most often seen in females. However, sensitive males sometimes let the tears flow too. Tears are usually caused by an emotional upheaval which causes sadness, but sometimes happiness causes tears of joy. When tears flow heavily, they are called *sobs*. Sobs cause people to:

"Cry buckets full!"

"Open the flood gates!"

"Cry rivers of tears!

If fat cells happen to experience sobs, hang on for dear life otherwise you may be washed away! Hopefully, it will not take long for you to dry out. Eventually, the human will run out of tears and you will only have to step around small puddles!

Attention fat cells who serve in the eyes! Whether your human has 20/20 vision or compromised eyesight, you must help them see things in the *right light*. What is this elusive right light? Fat cells are not certain of the meaning of this catchy anecdotal phrase. However, most fat cells think it means a human's ability to use their instinct to steer them in the right direction. That would be towards the kitchen! Right? Yes, that sounds good to fat cells! While humans are in the kitchen, here is a list of goals they should *read* and try to fulfill:

"A pantry stocked with nutritious food!"

"A hidden cache of chocolate for emergencies (Pleeeease)!"

" Cookbooks and joke books!"

"A list of all the Five Star restaurants they want to visit."

As far as fat cells are concerned, humans who fulfill these goals are on the right track. The *food track*!

If it seems we are hammering home lessons about food into your fat cell heads, then pound, pound, pound! We are! You are fat cells. This is your life! The purpose of this entire set of lessons is to educate you. It is imperative fat cells and cellulite cells keep humans alive.

Here is a credo: "Fat cells help the humans see, by serving them willingly!"

The Human Ears

Attention all fat cells! Listen up and lend us an ear! Actually, lend us two! This is a good time to remember what the philosopher *Fatpictetus* said: "With two ears and only one mouth, it is obvious we need to listen more!"

It is very true all fat cells need to practice the art of listening. Listen now as we give you an earful of advice about human ears! The ears may not be the prettiest parts of humans, but they are two of the most important. The gift of hearing is truly one of the greatest gifts God bestowed upon humans.

Many fat cells think the ears are just *one way* mechanisms used for hearing. They are much more than that. The ears are mechanical marvels which aid humans as they speak. How else are they going to tell each other jokes? Most jokes start out with the phrase: "Did you hear the one about…?" Those six words cause a unique reaction in human ears. Their ears ready themselves to hear the punch line and then great fits of laughter erupt! Yippee! Humans who make other humans laugh are like angels on earth! They make fat cells want to jump for joy!

Fat cells in the ears are mainly in the earlobes. They are one of the most coveted spots for fat cells. While there, they will hear giggles, chuckles and laughter! These sounds are music to fat cells' ears.

Without ears, humans could not have created music. As far as fat cells are concerned, music is like the beat of the heart; its tempo keeps humans going. When humans heard the proverbial *musical beat,* they realized there was more to communication than the spoken word. Thanks to those geniuses, musical notes and musical instruments were invented.

Music added a whole new dimension to the intelligence of humans. As Fatwig van Fathoven said: "You receive the ultimate in wisdom when you hear music!"

Fat cells believe humans would be lost without music. Music has been used to soothe a sorry soul, teach a lesson, encourage freedom, proclaim love, combat loneliness, announce a victory, celebrate a birth, lessen the sadness of a death, celebrate life and encourage religious beliefs.

Fat cells cannot forget the different forms of dance which were inspired by music. When humans dance, their appetites start to dance too. It is only a matter of time before their stomachs growl. Listen to that sound! Could cooking be on the horizon? Strike up the pans maestro! Here comes the sensational symphonic sounds of pots and pans clanging and banging. Soon the humans will eat and replenish the fat cells' lipid levels. Yippee!

Listen carefully as we continue to give fat cells an earful of education! Humans go through trials and tribulations on a daily basis. Most of them are imbued with skillful and analytical minds. However, all humans need a variety of emotions to cope with all the crap that's thrown their way. Thank goodness humans have emotions. If they did not, humans would act like robots and refuse to eat. Fat cells would be sunk! Boy does that send a shiver down our spines! When fat cells are serving a rotation in the ears, their humans may display extreme emotions. Fat cells need not be alarmed. If they accept the humans' rantings and ravings as part of the general insanity of humankind, fat cells will be okay.

Generally speaking, fat cells love to hear the spoken word. Humans sound special when they whisper. It is scary when they shout! Hopefully, you will hear a human sing. Fat cells may hear words of love spoken tenderly, menacing words spoken angrily, educational words spoken eloquently and profane words spoken carelessly! We have heard some fat cells swear, and damn it… we don't like it!

If fat cells hear a human say they are going to get their ears pierced, immediately alert a fat cell guard! They will try to move you to a safe location while the ears are being pierced. If the human decides to go crazy and pierce several areas up and down the ears, run for your lives! It will be hard as hell for us to rescue all of you! Go to the neck and stay there. We are sorry to put you in this predicament. For those fat cells who meet a tragic end, you will not be forgotten! Your names will be inscribed on plaques and displayed in the Fatistotle Cellulite Cell Charm Center. We give thanks to all fat cells (living or dead) for their service in the ears.

We must let fat cells know, many humans consider the ear lobes to be receptors for sensual overtures. In other words, some humans like to suck on each others' earlobes. We do not know why the humans do this, but if they are hungry we suggest they eat some food!

Here is a credo for fat cells: "When you are in the human's ear, we hope you love what you hear!"

The Human Nose

It's as plain as the nose on a human's face; the nose comes in all shapes and sizes. Fat cells agree the nose is an excellent tool for detecting odors and especially for... breathing!

Of course one of the greatest purposes of the nose is to smell food. After thousands of years of smelling swampy, muddy cave-human food, modern humans succeeded in developing foods that smelled good. Much to their noses and fat cells delight! When aromas from foods perfume the air, human appetites perk up. During the course of a day, humans smell dozens of different types of foods. These smells cause humans to think about eating! Yea! Fat cells will take all the help they can get! It is wonderful that tantalizing odors aid fat cells.

We must tell you, in spite of its scent service, a great deal of notoriety surrounds the human nose. Believe us, some fat cells are reluctant to go there! They are afraid of the sniffling, sneezing and snot snorting that goes on in the human nose. And where do all the boogers go? Yuck! You don't want to know! "Nobody nose. . . er. . . knows the trouble we've smelled!"

Regardless of their reluctance, fat cells have to go where they are needed. At some point in time, the nose could be their destination. Evidently, there is a curious situation in which the human nose swells to gigantic proportions. This malady is called *rhinophyma*. Fat cells refer to this condition as the *curiosity of nasal bulbousity*. When this malady occurs extra fat cells will be required in the nose to provide insulation. Fat cells must not feel guilty or self conscious if the human's nose becomes bulbous. They are doing what is needed. Fat cells will have to vie for position with blood vessels and questionable goo. It is advisable for them to summon all the stamina they possess and hang on for dear life! For those fat cells who have endured an episode of nasal bulbousity, please do not discuss your time spent in the nose with other fat cells.

Your comments may scare them into rebellious behavior! We want to avoid rallies filled with rioting rebels. Recently, an alarming placard was found hidden behind a pillar at the Fatistotle Cellulite Cell Charm Center. It said: "Fat Cells Against Nefarious Nasal Duties."

Please do not engage in reckless behavior and run the risk of endangering other fat cells. Anarchists will be dealt with swiftly. Rebel fat cells will immediately be taken to the Anarchy Reformation Chamber and brainwashed into acceptable behavior. The rebel fat cells will endure mitochondrial manipulation and lipid leaching. If the traitors still show no remorse, fat cell guards will be instructed to escort them to the Feces Flow Dipping Vat. Do not risk it! It isn't worth it! Fecal matter is no laughing matter! If other fat cells ask about your stay in the human nose, tell them to quit being so *nosey*. Please try to fulfill your nasal duties with grace and charm.

Remember the famous fat cell credo: "When the nose puts us to the test, fat cells are at their best!"

The Human Neck

The neck is one of the most significant parts of the human body because it holds up the head where all the crazy ideas hide out. Which is fine with us! Crazy ideas often lead to hunger and food consumption! Yea! Fat cells want humans to keep those thoughts of food flowing! The more humans eat the better we feel... uh. . . we mean the better they feel!

Fat cells provide pillars of support in the neck. However, cellulite cells occasionally serve in an unusual neck structure called the *dewlap*. The dewlap is a strange looking phenomenon which hangs down beneath some human chins. Some people call it a *turkey neck*! Not the fat cells! We think it is kind of fun to hang out there. It is one of the fat cells easiest rotation locations.

Most humans have beautiful necks! Many fat cells think the neck is a very sensual part of the human body. We like to call it a *kissing neck*! Most humans love to kiss each others necks. They even have a name for this behavior: *Necking*! Humans are very playful when they neck. They kiss, laugh and kiss some more! We hope all fat cells have a chance to observe an episode of humans necking. However, remember our rules! If humans become too frisky, close your eyes and cover your fat cell ears!

Remember this credo: "Fat cells serve the neck well, they help make it really swell!"

The Female Human Breasts

Fat cells reign supreme in the female breasts. Yes, yes, we are needed! We are even desired in this area! Finally some recognition for fat cells! There is no denying the importance of fat cells in the female breasts. Without the breasts, humans would not have survived. Millions of humans were nourished by these fat filled glands. The female breasts have been revered throughout history, and fat cells share this history with them. We are humble and proud of our service in the female breasts.

Traditionally, this area has been served by ancestral breast fat cells. Breast fat cells are extraordinary! Many of them carry ancestral secrets which were whispered to them in hushed and hurried ways. Those secrets were passed down to direct descendants and never revealed to outsiders.

With the introduction of Fatistotle's program, many cellulite cells were placed in female breasts. Ancestral breast fat cells graciously allowed cellulite cells to join them. This tradition continues, and we must insist that all cellulite cells show respect to the ancestral breast fat cells. As time passes, you will have a mutual appreciation for one another.

Cellulite cells, please pay special attention to the following information. We must discuss the physical and psychological ways in which you will be affected during your rotation in female breasts. Many cellulite cells have a history of service in non-challenged areas. We do not intend to belittle you by this statement. As you know in the thighs, abdomens or buttocks, cellulite cells were allowed to hang around in a leisurely manner. We know some of you were tortured and put through cellulite hell when females tried to rid themselves of you; we are sorry for that. There is help available for the cellulite cells who were tortured. We are happy to announce the creation of a new committee called the Cellulite Cell Calming and Coping Council. The council consists of specially trained cellulite cells who will help you with any of your lingering problems and/or neuroses. We must advise you, do not abuse the committee's assistance. Do not claim to have problems when none exist! We have ways to ferret out cellulite cells that misrepresent themselves. It is essential for us to work together harmoniously. Any cellulite cells who cause a disruption in our routine, will be punished! They will undergo (yes... you guessed it) repeated dips in the Feces Flow Dipping Vat!

For those fat cells who have recently served a rotation in a more casual area, please pay attention! You are in for a tremendous change. When a female human has a baby, she experiences many emotions. She may feel the following: anxiety, tenderness, happiness, sadness and love!

All cellulite cells must maintain their full, swollen selves while in the breasts. Your female will need your full support as she navigates these emotions. This will not be an easy assignment for cellulite cells. However, there will be times when you feel relaxed and happy. When baby humans suckle at their Mothers' breasts, cellulite cells will feel their love and tenderness. You may physically swell with happiness while watching their delicate interaction. Remember it well! With the passage of time, the baby humans will grow into something called *teenagers*. The tender actions between Mother and child may go from tenderness to *TNT*!

Talk about *personutilties*! Some of these young humans are nutty enough to warrant their own species! Watch out! Adult female humans may feel as though they are running through exploding mine fields when dealing with teenagers. This may be a very stressful time for the Mothers.

All fat cells in the breasts must keep an eye on their lipid levels. Female humans may have periods of sadness due to fluctuations in their estrogen levels. This is not the time for cellulite cells to feel sorry for themselves. As you know, ancestral breast fat cells have been dealing with these female human emotions for centuries. While in the female breasts, cellulite cells must have total dedication and concentration.

Your coping skills will be further utilized as you become familiar with a contraption called the *brassiere*. The brassiere, also called a *bra*, was designed to capture and entrap the female breasts. Most female humans wear bras. Most male humans want to take them off of the females. Some males are obsessed with female breasts and talk about them constantly. They refer to female breasts by all kinds of strange names such as: *boobs*, *tits*, *knockers*, *gazongas*, *jugs* and *hooters*. They try to touch them constantly! When the males are not touching them, they think about touching them! Some males huddle together in groups and say things such as:

"Get a load of those knockers!"

"Did you see those big boobs?"

"Boy, she's got humongous jugs!"

This *boob insanity* continues with males' fascination with the size of the breasts. As far as some of them are concerned, the bigger the boobs the better! Thanks to cultural craziness, ideal measurements have been assigned to determine the optimum sizes for certain female body parts. The female breasts are the first body parts in a group of three that undergo what fat cells call a *measurement assessment*. The other two body parts will be discussed later. The measurement of the female breasts is especially significant for fat cells. The number which is often used as an ideal size for female breasts is 36 inches. However, many humans clamor for larger breasts. Since fat cells help to enlarge the female breasts, they feel needed and appreciated there. Most humans like the way fat cells turn the breasts into large round mounds. It seems the bigger the female breasts are, the more excited the males become. This goes to show, some male humans often act like *boobs* when it comes to the female boobs. However, most female humans seem to enjoy the attention. Fat cells feel it is important to point out, whether big or small, they think all female breasts are beautiful!

As to the *containment contraption/torture device* known as

the. . . brassiere, fat cells do not like it. Most fat cells believe it should be called the *squashiere* since it squashes the hell out of them! We caution all breast fat cells to be considerate of their sister fat cells when they are crammed up against one another in a brassiere. We know you feel like sardines in a can, but this is not the time to act like uppity prima donnas. No one ever said it was easy to be a fat cell. Just try to plump up and stay firm. Fortunately, most females take their bras off when they sleep. Fat cells should retain their positions until the females remove their bras. At this point, you may breathe a sigh of relief, stretch out and relax!

Please be advised the bra can cause heat to develop within fat cells. This may cause their lipids to become a dark color, and they may emit odors. This is an emergency! Please go to the Lipid Recirculation Chamber for prompt medical attention. Most fat cells should be able to return to their duties within twenty-four hours or less.

While serving in the female breasts, some fat cells may encounter an unusual situation. The following announcement may shock you! Let it be known, some female cellulite cells contain the male hormone *testosterone*! This may cause some of them to act in a masculine manner. We will not tolerate testosterone laden cellulite cells harassing female ancestral breast fat cells! These cellulite cells will not make vulgar comments such as:

"Did you see the size of those jugs!"

"Look at those knockers!"

"I want to tweak those titties!"

Many newcomers do not understand the wonder which surrounds the ancestral breast fat cells. They deserve our respect, and they shall receive it!

Please pay special attention to the following rule. The areola area of the female breasts which encircles the nipples will only be filled by ancestral breast fat cells! Cellulite cells cannot spend time there! Do not try to trick the ancestral breast fat cells into switching places with you. Their nuclei

45

are on high alert for suspicious activity. Let it be known: "OFFENDERS WILL BE CAUGHT!" These cellulite cells will be hauled away by fat cell guards and delivered to the Feces Flow Dipping Vat! After several dunks, the offending cellulite cells will never harass ancestral breast fat cells again!

Please remember this ancient fat cell credo: "Ancestral breast fat cells know, they help the human milk to flow!"

The Human Heart

Fat cells believe the heart is the most unique of all human organs. Most humans consider their brains the command centers of their bodies. From what fat cells can tell after thousands of years of service to humans, their hearts and brains are almost equal.

The heart is mainly muscle tissue in terms of its physical structure. Fat cells located in the heart are called visceral fat cells. They are there to provide protection. Most fat cells will never see the heart, but make no mistake they will hear a lot about it.

The heart is a practical unit which says: *lub dupp, lub dupp* to doctors and scientists as it laboriously beats while doing its job. Wrong! Fat cells know the truth! The heart really says: *love dove, love dove*! The steady heartbeat reminds humans they need love. The dove is thrown in for good measure since humans love symbols. Speaking of symbols, the traditional shape of a red heart is known worldwide. Fat cells are thrilled a human invented the heart shaped box which holds Valentine candies. What a joyous combination, love and candy! Just think, it's as though it was made for fat cells!

Most fat cells appreciate the ease in which humans fall in love. When they have love in their hearts, humans are happy. It certainly helps fat cells too! Humans love to eat when they are in love! Some humans even say, the way to a man's heart is through his stomach. They also use the word love to express their appreciation for food. Here are some things fat cells have heard humans say about food:

"Mom, I love your cooking!"

"I love pizza!"

"I love candy so much I could eat the whole box!"

Isn't it remarkable! Not only do humans love each other, they can have a love affair with food too. . . especially candy!

No one knows exactly what happens when humans fall in love or why it seems easy for them to do so. However, there are some skeptical fat cells who think some humans are reluctant to fall in love. These fat cells believe *love doctors* need to research the true meaning of falling in love. They think the investigation should start with humans' DNA. These skeptics believe hidden deep within the DNA lies a unique ancient defense mechanism called the *flight or fight reflex.* While referring only to the *flight* aspect of the reflex, the skeptical fat cells think some humans are afraid to fall in love and may actually flee when they feel love is closing in on them. The fact that these humans feel love is dangerous reflects the power of the flight reflex. Some examples of intense flight reflex follow:

"What was that sound? Oh no, love is in the air? I've got to get the hell out of here!

"My heart is pounding, it may be love! I better getaway before it's too late! Where's the exit?"

"She's got the look of love in her eyes! I'm out of here!"
Some doubting fat cells are willing to concede, most human hearts may be able to override the flight reflex. This could explain how so many humans fall in love. With their guards down, humans are able to seek and give affection. As they throw caution to the wind and happily cavort about, humans fall in love. Dumbfounded and awestruck with wonder, the humans never knew what hit them!

Other fat cells paint a different picture of *love's* capture of humans. While lonely humans wander endlessly searching for love, fat cupids with quivers full of arrows throng the air. When the time is right, fat cupids let their arrows fly. They rain down upon humans like silvery bolts of passion! Zap! Zap! Zap!

"Ow, something just hit me in my ass!" shouts a human. Other love struck humans with looks of wonder on their faces, turn to those near them and say, *I love you*! Yes that proves it, *love does make the world go around*!

Fat cells have to admit both love scenarios described above have merit. However, a resounding number of fat cells agree, the idea of fat cupids tickles them pink!

Whether humans are falling in love or not, fat cells have to get to the *heart of the matter.* Many fat cells believe the heart is the perfect host for humans' feelings of love. However, we do not want those lovey-dovey emotions to interfere with humans' feelings of hunger. Hunger pangs are part of the body's quest for proper *homeostasis.* Fat cells believe since eating is essential for humans' survival, it is logical that humans' heartfelt feelings lead them toward the preparation of food. Thanks to the inventors of all types of cooking tools and kitchenware, most humans become proficient cooks. Many fat cells believe passionate humans who have *big hearts* often possess culinary creativity. Humans should let their hearts lead the way and dine on nutritious foods. Good nutrition helps humans to have good heart health.

As humans race toward preparing delicious foods, we are proud to be their little fat cell drivers! We know humans need us for bursts of energy for their creativity!

Here is a credo for all fat cells: "Fat cells help the heart to beat, we think that is really neat!"

The Male Human Breasts

Males do not want large fatty breasts. They want flat muscular chests! Males want to be manly with medals upon their chests not big boobs!

There is a situation in which some males develop big breasts. All male humans have a small amount of the female hormone *estrogen* in their bodies. Sometimes their estrogen levels rise, and they grow bigger breasts. At this time extra fat cells can be found there. Warning! We must tell you this, and we will not mince words:

"EXTRA FAT CELLS ARE NOT WELCOME IN MALE BREASTS!"

The fleshy, breasted males will use every avenue available to rid themselves of extra fat cells. Many of them will lift weights to encourage muscle development. With extra muscle cells swaggering around, fat cells will have to struggle to maintain their positions. Unfortunately, some of you may feel as though you have been run over by steam rollers. Please try to retain your proper fat cellular shapes. Gather into large groups and bounce yourselves off the muscle cells! This will startle them and give fat cells an advantage. Hopefully, confusion will ensue, and the muscle cells will retreat. Stay in your fat cell groups; there is strength in numbers! Whatever you do, don't run screaming for an exit. None exists! You're stuck, so stick it out. Maintain your plumpness and act defiant. Once the muscle cells see that fat cells cannot be undone, they will back off!

Fat cells realize muscle cells have jobs to do. We appreciate the physical support they provide for fat cells. However, we protect them from blows and other external harm. Please remember all fat cells have the right to be in male breasts.

A strict code of conduct exists for fat cells who reside in male breasts. They must behave in a civil manner. We have heard tales of outlandish behavior in this area. Do not call your male human a *twit with tits*! Do not say he has *man boobs*! Do not proclaim he needs a bra. And for Pete's sake, do not say he has *bitch tits*! Insensitive fat cells who behave in a cloddish manner will be taken to the Feces Flow Dipping Vat. After hours of agony, we assure you those fat cells will regret their rude behavior!

Here is a credo you can use to help unnerve the muscle cells: "Believe us when we say, fat cells are here to stay!"

The Human Underarms

Attention all fat cells! Please do not recoil in horror as we educate you about fleshy underarm tissue. Thanks to the advent of perfumes and deodorants, the underarms usually are bearable. This is a very significant area for all fat cells.

We know God proclaimed humans must have laughter. Some of our illustrious fat cell nuclei believe the locations under the arms prove a true physical connection between God and humans. For you see, humans conduct an action in this area called *tickling*! Tickling causes great fits of laughter in most humans. Several of our fat cells experienced tickling while on duty in the underarms. Many of them had the *giggles* for hours afterwards. Most fat cells believe this shows irrefutable proof of the connection between God, humans and laughter. Thanks to this belief, most fat cells do not mind duty in the underarms!

However, some of you do not like this area. This is common among fat cells who have spent time encased within stinky sticky underarm tissue. Some humans refuse to wear deodorant and may be very smelly. Yuck! We're talking about stench with a capital *S*! The stench is so odiferous, it could cause a carcass to rise from the dead and run away! This kind of body odor could take down a twenty ton brontosaurus! Fat cells have seen pollution advisories issued because of those stinky humans. There have been times when humans wearing gas masks have had to fumigate areas after those stinkers left. Whatever their reasons, humans who fail to properly attend to their malodorous underarms cause problems for fat cells.

Most fat cells are tough, tolerant power-balls of pudginess. However, there are some who have a low level of tolerance for foul odors. Those fat cells anxiously rub their cell linings as they attempt to rid themselves of their human's noxious odors. During their rubbing mania, they often bump up against nearby fat cells. Their *fume phobias* do not end there. As the choking fat cells strive for cleaner air, their coughing drives other fat cells nuts. Fat cells call this, a *fume frenzy*, and it is not pretty to watch. Fights have broken out between fat cells fending off fume phobias!

Fat cells are not the collective moral conscience of humans. Thank the good Lord above for that! However, fat cells have to live in humans. Enough is enough! What's with you stinky humans? Haven't you heard of *green house gasses*? Your funky fumes are not helping matters. You cannot always slide under the radar! If it were up to fat cells, we would plunge you stinkers into tubs full of soapy bubbles and scrub you raw. We beg you to use the bath products invented by your fellow humans. Soap and perfume go a long way in stifling body odor pollution. . . thank goodness!

Here is a coping credo for fat cells and cellulite cells: "Even though some humans smell, fat cells perform their duties well!"

The Human Funny
Bone/Humerus

Make no *bones* about it, humans can be very comical! At least that is how they act after whacking their *funny bones*! The humans' responses are instantaneous. They grab their elbows and thrash around madly gyrating to and fro. Fat cells think this explains the origin of *modern dance*! The humans movements are wild and hilarious! Everyone else laughs at them and sometimes they even laugh at themselves.

Whether it is comedy or modern dance, humans have two funny bones; one in each upper arm. It was ingenious of God to give them two of these bones. If the humans avoid hitting one, they always have a chance to hit the other. You know fat cells, they love to hear laughter! Speaking of laughter, it is quite *humorous* that the funny bone is medically called the *humerus*! We forgive the scientists for misspelling the word!

With regards to fat cells, we hope they have a humorous time when on duty near the humerus.

Credo of fun: "The humerus bone provides fun when humans hit one!"

The Human Forearms

The forearms are extremely important because they are connected to the magnificent human hands. There are two bones in each forearm. They are called the ulna and the radius. The radius is the larger of the two bones and holds the most importance for fat cells. Generally speaking, most humans do not have a lot of fat cells in their forearms. However, one of our most important and unique fat cells resides there. He is known as the *Radial Raconteur.* The Radial Raconteur is a metaphysical enigma that takes the form of a fat cell. He is in one forearm of every human, male and female alike.

Fat cells are not sure how he survived through the ages. The Radial Raconteur is a kind and gentle soul. He is a thespian, a poet, an artist and a musician.

If and when any fat cells serve a rotation near the radius, please give the Radial Raconteur the respect he deserves. If a fat cell is caught being disrespectful to him, the offender will suffer a severe punishment. Over the years we have amassed a wonderful collection of the Radial Raconteur's work. We have included a nice selection of his writings for your reading pleasure and enjoyment.

The Radial Raconteur

I am the Radial Raconteur,
you may call me Monsieur.
My motives are always pure,
of this you can be sure.

It is in my fat cell nature,
to sing songs for my own pleasure.
I have many tunes I treasure,
so I sing them at my leisure.

A Short Ode to the Radius

The radius deserves a pleasant ode,
it is a tale that should be told.
The Raconteur must be mighty and bold
because it is a bone he has to hold.

Flourish

The human lifts his fork with a flourish,
to his lips so he might nourish,
with foods he does cherish,
he takes in sustenance so he will not perish.

Kingly Throne

I sit upon my throne,
down here all alone.
It's not my fate I bemoan,
I need a queen to call my own.

The Human Hands

Human hands are without a doubt, two of the most marvelous creations of all times. Thanks to fat cells, they are exquisite instruments. For you see, without the finger and palm fat pads, the hands would just be skin and bones painfully hitting against whatever they touch. Ouch! Thankfully for humans, fat cells literally have all human hands in the palms of their hands!

Even though fat cells undergo a tremendous amount of physical stress in this area, they love human hands. Fat cells have had a hand in all the humans' creations. Yes, we have to hand it to humans, they are always willing to work and create using their hands. Most humans prefer to stay busy. Generally speaking, they do not like to sit around and twiddle their thumbs. For those fat cells who have not served in a high stress area, be prepared for an extraordinary experience! As fat cells cushion and secure the hands, they will witness remarkable things.

Fat cells will also learn first hand the meaning of insanity. Humans use their hands all day long and sometimes forget to use their brains! This is when accidents happen! Fat cells should prepare themselves to experience a smorgasbord of swear words! The curse words really fly when humans injure their hands!

It seems humans have invented thousands of ways to compromise their hands. Fat cells are not referring to basic inventions which help humans. We are talking about crazy things that blow off fingers! Like firecrackers! Fat cells feel compelled to say:

"Stop it humans, there are fat cells inside your fingers, and they do not want to go flying off in all directions!"

Humans did not stop with firecrackers! Some handy humans invented another item which threatens fat cells. *Stupor glue*! What's with that stuff? Some humans cannot pry their fingers apart for hours after using it. Speaking of glue, we wish female humans would consider the health of fat cells when they have fake nails applied to their fingertips. Hello! There are fat cells in there who are in danger of suffocating! Since we are on the subject of suffocating, it would be greatly appreciated if humans would buy new rubber gloves once in a while. The smell inside old gloves is enough to gag a maggot!

Attention fat cells, when you serve your first rotation in the hands, please anchor yourself against another fat cell who has experience in the area. Please try your best to accommodate your fellow fat cells. Maintain your composure! Do not let things get out of hand! Cross your fingers and hope that all fat cells will do a fine job while they are in the hands!

Our service to human hands has been a monumental success. In honor of all fat cells, we asked each of them to write a thoughtful comment about the time they spent in the fingers or hands. We received replies from thousands of fat cells. Regretfully, there was not enough room to showcase all of them here. To view the rest of them, go to the Fatistotle Cellulite Cell Charm Center. Here are some of the comments:

"I glowed when I felt the soft caress of a Mother touching her newborn child."

"A snowflake upon a child's fingertip gave me a cool tingle."

"I felt as though I was part of a violin when a male coaxed it into surrendering the notes of a song."

"I was an artist for a moment when I helped to hold the brush as a painter filled a canvass with color."

"My cell was filled with glee when a human and I tickled the ivories on a grand piano."

"I was enthralled with the skill of a neurosurgeon's fingers when he saved a human's life."

"Love flowed around me as I held the pen when a lover wrote a message to his dearly beloved."

"I felt the pride of a Father when he patted his son on the back for a job well done."

"I led the orchestra when a conductor waved his baton."

"I sowed the seeds and helped reap the harvest from a fruitful vegetable garden."

"The bells rang triumphantly as I helped to ring them in an old European cathedral."

"A dog's fur tickled me when a human lovingly petted it."

"I marveled at the skill in a scientist's hands when she used an electron microscope."

"Immediate happiness filled me when I helped a child hold a kite that was flying high above us."

"My cell was lipid weary but happy when a human finished typing her first book."

"I was thrilled to hold the needle when a female embroidered a beautiful linen table cloth."

"My fingers danced over a map as a teacher pointed out the constellations to a classroom full of students."

"A male human was filled with confidence as I helped to grasp the football tightly when he scored a touchdown."

"I felt a great tenderness as a human caressed a kitten."

"My cell felt gooey as a female kneaded dough to make bread."

"It was exhilarating when a human lovingly caressed his soul mate."

"I felt slippery when a female molded clay on her potter's wheel."

"I became one with the instrument when a male strummed his guitar."

"I felt like a technician when I helped assemble a new computer."

Credo of encouragement: "Fat cells meet all demands while in the human hands!"

The Human Abdomen/Belly

The abdominal area or belly is in the front part of the human torso. It is below the breasts and slightly above the pubic area. The belly is a prime location for fat cells. In fact it is teeming with them! Some human bellies are double-teeming or even triple-teeming with fat cells! Because of overcrowding, one or two fat cells may be misplaced. Do not worry, we eventually find them all!

Generally speaking, the belly is a great place for fat cells. Many humans seem to have acceptance of their large abdomens. Some humans with big bellies engage in comedic acts with one another. These comedians are well received and cause other humans to laugh at their stunts. They even created a phrase to describe the laughter that comes from deep within them. It is called the *belly-laugh*! Yippee! Fat cells love laughter! We believe the coined phrase belly-laugh proves the humans' acceptance of extra fat cells in their bellies. Whatever size their bellies are, whether big, small or in between, fat cells thank comedians for making us laugh.

Fat cells in the abdomen seem to be evenly distributed between males and females. Males with excessive belly fat are said to have *beer bellies* or *spare tires*. They also joke and laugh about an area called the *love handles*! Whereas in females, words like *roly poly* or *jelly belly* may be used to describe their belly fat.

Fat cells must be prepared to experience some interesting activities when in the belly area. When females *belly dance,* fat cells may feel as though they are bouncing upon the ocean. The abdomen goes up and down, up and down! It's enough to make fat cells seasick! It's worth the effort though because vigorous dancing is an excellent exercise for humans.

Another activity called *stumo* wrestling involves gigantic males wearing something similar to cloth diapers. They smack their huge bellies together over and over again with tremendous force. When these pounding crashes occur, all hell breaks loose among the fat cells in the belly. This situation turns into a horrible nightmare with fat cells running in all directions. Unfortunately, during the stampede, many fat cells are displaced. Eventually, one of the wrestlers is declared a winner and the stumo match ends. With the help of fat cell guards, the misplaced fat cells re-group and attend to their duties in the belly. Fortunately, most humans do not want to run around in cloth diapers and engage in this type of activity.

In regards to female humans, most of them refer to the belly area as the waist, and they want it to be small. Many of them spend hours talking about how small their waists should be. The waist is the second prominent area of the female which undergoes a measurement assessment. The breasts are first, followed by the waist and then the buttocks/ass. When the numbers are right, this trio of measurements is commonly referred to as an *hour glass figure*! Because of pressures from society, many females worry about having the perfect shape. When they are not worrying about their breasts or asses, females are worrying about their waists. Many of them complain to each other about the size of their waists. When females tire of hearing the complaints, they say:

"Quit your *belly-aching*!"

This is an excellent example of the way humans communicate with one another. We love the phrase, *quit your belly-aching*! For those fat cells who serve time in the belly, maintain your cellular shapes and do not complain. In other words, *quit your belly-aching* and do the job that is required of you!

Fat cells beware! Many humans encircle the abdominal area with a leather strap called a belt. When some humans sit down, mounds of fat spill over their belts. Unfortunately, many fat cells feel intense pressure when this happens. Please try not to squirm! It is essential for fat cells who are under cellulite cells to maintain their positions. We know some fat cells still have disdain for cellulite cells. Do not try to deny it! Put your resentment aside and maintain your fat selves. **Do not allow a cellulite cell collapse!** If a cellulite cell collapse occurs, the human's belly may have uneven pockets of fat. Numerous lumps and bumps could appear in the belly which could be catastrophic for fat cells! There have been cases when cellulite cell collapses have triggered. . . *liposuction*! Liposuction is fatal for fat cells. FAT CELLS DO NOT COME BACK!

When some humans look into their mirrors and see uneven layers of fat tissue, they become horrified. They seek help from a doctor called a plastic surgeon. After the doctor receives a large monetary payment, he sucks the human's fat into a monstrously, scary *liposuction machine*. After the fat is collected, it is squashed and dried. Fat cells think humans add some resin to it and turn it into plastic bottles. Fat cells believe that is why these doctors are called *plastic surgeons*.

We do not want liposuction to be performed on any fat cells! Years ago we received a report from a female fat cell guard. She was on patrol in the upper area of a female human when liposuction was performed on her human's belly. The guard said the death screams coming from her fellow cellulite cells still echo through her brain. She is tortured to this day because there was no way for her to save them. The female fat cell guard wears a shroud of guilt like a heavy cloak. It is a cloak which will never be removed.

Please be advised, one of our artistic cellulite cells created a button which reads, "Down With Liposuction, It *Sucks*!"
Fat cells who want a button, may pick up one at the Fatistotle Cellulite Cell Curriculum Center.

Here is an appropriate credo meant to bolster cellulite cells while they are in the abdominal area: "Even when cellulite cells wiggle like jelly, they're thrilled to be in the belly!"

The Human Penis

The male human reproductive organ is called the penis. Fat cells do not have penises. Thank God for that! We were not sure what to tell fat cells about the penis. There were many heated discussions about this organ. Perhaps we should have said *or-gone* instead of organ since many men have *gone* completely crazy due to this dangling appendage! Some fat cell administrators walked out of the Fatistotle Cellulite Cell Curriculum Center when we began discussion of the penis. The fat cell administrators said they did not want to talk about it! Oh yeah? Well who does? We do, that's who! We are not going to let a little or big thing (which ever the case may be) such as the penis stop us from educating our fellow fat cells.

We feel it is essential for you to know about all areas of the human body. Fat cells deserve to know what they will be up against. Since the penis abuts up to the pubis, fat cells literally will be up against the penis when they serve rotational pubic duty. Fat cells should not be alarmed if they start to feel crazy. Crazy does not begin to describe the insanity which surrounds this organ!

After scratching our little fat heads and wringing our hands, we decided to have a talk with the *big boss*. Even though we knew he would not have time to give us any answers, we couldn't help but ask him some questions about the penis:

"God, what were you thinking?"

"Did you have a little too much wine that day?"

"Couldn't you have put an automatic shut off valve on that thing?"

"Honestly, was it really wise to put that thing in a pair of pants?"

"Why does it keep trying to pop back out?"

"Why doesn't the zipper stay zipped?"

For those fat cells who are unfamiliar with the penis, it is a long shaft with a meaty tip at the end called the *glans*. We are not sure if there are any fat cells in the glans. We are all too afraid to go down there and look! If there are any fat cells down there, they are on their own! We know fat cells have been instructed to cooperate and stick together. Not there! We don't want to sticky to a dicky! It's too tricky! Fat cells don't mean to whine, but the penis is the scariest part of male humans.

Most male humans call the tip of their penis the *head*. Sometimes it seems this head does <u>all</u> their thinking for them. Maybe this explains why so many males do not think with their other head (you know... their brain)! As fat cells know, some male humans call the penis the *dick*. This could explain phrases such as:

"He thinks with his dick!"

"He's a dick head!"

When the male thinks of his dick, his thought processes go wild! The average adult male may think of his penis every thirty seconds. Let us clarify further; he thinks of using it for the purpose of sex! Sex is the term used by humans to describe the mating ritual which may or may not facilitate human reproduction. Since the male thinks of sex every thirty seconds, he is under what fat cells call a, *sex hex*. The male cannot stop thinking about his penis, and he has a lot of questions about it:

"Is it big enough?"

"Where should I put it?"

"How long should I leave it there?"

"Do I put it there often enough?"

"Could it fall off from lack of use?"

"Could it fall off from over use?"

That question sends a shiver down the male human's spine. He quickly touches his penis to make sure it is there. His penis's response may sound something like this:

"I'm still here you idiot!"

"I want sex now you moron!"

"Man, what are you waiting for?"

"You want it, you know you want it!"

"I want to get laid!"

"Masturbation sucks buddy!"

At this point, the exasperated male screams:

"Shut up you little prick!

"I'll have sex when I'm good and ready!"

The penis's response:

"That's what you said three months ago... you dick head!"

As you can see, some males let their penises do their thinking for them. That is why fat cells call it a *sex hex*!

Many fat cells believe, no other organ has been as widely discussed as the male penis. The males seem to feel more powerful when they can joke and laugh about their dicks. They also have some other weird names for their penises. To some of the males it is a *cock*, to others it is a *joystick*! Other males refer to it as a *pecker* or a *wiener*!

Most male humans love to brag about their sexual escapades. Some males congregate around one another and chuckle as they brag about *getting laid, getting lucky* or *bagging a babe*. After hours of empty boasting, many of them return to their homes where they ponder the reality of their nonexistent sex lives! In all fairness, we feel fat cells should know, not all males behave in this manner. Those who are in touch with their feminine side are almost. . . human! Just kidding, of course. . . they are human too!

Here is a naughty credo for fat cells: "Watch out for the *dicky*, it can be *tricky*!"

The Human Scrotum

The scrotal sac or the scrotum is a bashful sensitive part of the male human anatomy. From what fat cells can tell, it just wants to be left alone. Who can blame the poor scrotum, its boss is the penis! Look out! When that thing stands at attention, it thinks everyone else should too! The shy, silent scrotum does not dare utter a sound. It knows it is in total servitude to its master. If that's not enough of a burden, the scrotum has to protect the *family jewels* too! What a responsibility!

Most males refer to the family jewels as the *balls* or *nuts*. The medical term for the nuts is the *gonads*. Instead of being labeled the gonads they should be called the *gonuts*! When it comes to their gonads, most males literally seem to go nuts! Some males scratch their scrotum and talk about their nuts endlessly. The balls are a hot topic when males discuss their interactions with females. Most of their comments about females are positive. However, at times some males become angry and slam females by saying things such as:

"She's a ball buster!"

"She's got me by the balls!"

"She's a real nutcracker!"

So you see, males are often driven nuts by their *nuts*!

Fat cells' duties in this nutty area will be minimal. Some of you will line the scrotal sac to act as buffers when the penis dangles and bangs against the scrotum.

Beware! This can be a sweaty stinky dangerous area. A fungal rash called *jock itch* sometimes occurs. As a result, male humans may vigorously scratch their scrotums. Fat cells will bear the direct brunt of the scratching. Do not shrink down and shirk your duties! Sooner or later the humans will receive treatment, and the scratching will end.

Here's a credo: "Balls and all, fat cells answer the call!"

The Human Mons Pubis

The mons pubis is one of the most important areas of the female body for fat cells. It is uh. . . er. . . a delicate area to talk about because it has to do with uh. . . er. . . sex!

Mons pubis is Latin for *mound of Venus*! Fat cells think it should be called the *fleshy fat mound* since they provide protective fat pads there.

Venus was the goddess of love. You know what that means, sex and lots of it! Hello horny humans! Wow! You really keep the fat cells busy in the fleshy fat mound! Fat cells have heard some weird noises while on duty there! In fact, this is the number one spot where fat cells demand ear plugs. Frankly, we often run out of them because of all the grunting and groaning!

Fat cells wonder why after all the wild antics and thrashing around, the humans call out: "Oh God, oh God? What about us, why don't the humans call out, Oh fat cells, oh fat cells? After all we provide the marvelous padding there!

Since fat cells rarely receive accolades, we want to take a moment to thank all fat cells who have bravely served in the mons pubis. We know many of you have suffered through relentless pounding. We our proud of your strength and fortitude! This is an area in which it is absolutely essential for fat cells to provide padding for comfort. You are literally helping with procreation. . . whether you want to or not! We are all for more humans! They keep fat cells in business!

Fat cells beware! Rumor has it some of you have spied on copulating humans. You should be ashamed of yourselves! Fat cells know spying is EXPRESSLY FORBIDDEN! Stop it now or the guilty parties will go for a dipping party at the Feces Flow Dipping Vat! Please remember all fat cells must strive to conduct themselves in a civil manner!

Here is a credo: "In the fleshy fat mound, fat cells abound!"

The Human Buttocks/Ass

Many humans around the world consider the buttocks/ass a thing of beauty. Proof of this exists in all the great works of art which showcase the fleshy buttocks of nude models. Fat cells believe the old masters captured the true essence of the human ass. Their paintings reveal the softness of the plump, round buttocks and are considered masterpieces.

We have to take a moment to explain something to all fat cells. During our years of service to humans, fat cells learned many words of slang. Ass is one such word. Fat cells know it sounds crude, but sometimes it is so artfully appropriate, we cannot help ourselves. Besides, humans use it so often it has become ingrained in fat cell lingo.

Thanks to fat cells, human buttocks are marvels of anatomical engineering. They turn the ass into a comfortable cushion when someone sits down on a hard wooden chair. Millions of fat cells willingly provide plump padding to cushion the vulnerable pelvic bones. Although fat cells and cellulite cells are often squashed beyond recognition while in the buttocks, they still strive to do a good job!

Fat cells have never met an ass they didn't like! They work in all varieties of human asses. Fat cells do not differentiate between *bulky butts, colossal cabooses* or *tiny tushies*. They are thrilled to be *fanny fat.*

Humans express admiration for their asses in many different ways. Male humans alter their voices in a pleasant way when they describe attractive female asses.

Some humans use humor to poke fun at other humans' asses. These individuals often share the same stage with the comedians who joke about the belly. They like to test their audience and often push the limit with their jokes. Human body parts are often the *butt* of jokes. There is nothing better to serve as the butt of a joke than the buttocks! Fat cells appreciate the comedians who focus on fat fannies. We love laughter as much as humans do. Here are some examples of the comedians jokes:

"When she walked into the room, her large ass ripped off the door jamb!"

"She has eaten so much candy the world's supply of sugar has dropped by 80%!"

"She has a sign on her ass that reads: "CAUTION: WIDE LOAD!"

Comedians are not the only ones who use the word ass. A huge segment of the human population seems to take great delight in using the word ass on a daily basis. It seems to be one of their favorite words. Some humans work it into their dialogues as often as possible with comments such as:

"She's a pain in the ass!"

"He's pain in the ass!"

"He's a real bad ass!"

"You can kiss my ass!"

In addition to those comments, there are humans who excel at using words in a weird way. The word ass is one such word. Only a human can take the ass, and transform it into a body part that can come off and move about. For example:

"Get your ass out of here!"

"Get your ass in here!"

"Get your ass out of bed!"

"Get your ass to school!"

Fat cells want to know, what happens to the rest of the body? Does it just stand there clutching at the area where the ass used to be? When does the ass come back? What if the ass wants to switch places with another human's ass? What if the ass travels to another country and asks for *ass asylum*? What if the ass attempts to run for political office? Nope, that won't work! Remember, that has already been tried by an ass! His behavior was crass because he was full of gas which made him sass until he came to an impasse when others took away his ability to harass by kicking him out on his ass! Whew! All that ass activity could put anyone into a state of agitation. Now do you see why fat cells say humans are nuts! This stuff goes on everyday! As fat cells can see, some humans have very complex relationships with their asses. It's why so many of them need chocolate! And lots of it with lots of variety! Fat cells hope humans have a good supply on hand!

Fat cells have come to realize that dire circumstances often exist between some female humans and their buttocks. Most of them do not want an ass the size of Texas! Some females harbor secret fears about their bulbous butts. Their fear becomes so severe they develop a syndrome fat cells call, *ACD (Ass Compulsion Disorder)!* ACD compels females to obsessively measure their asses. If the measurements reveal gigantic buttocks, the females' screams of anguish can be heard around the world! When their screams die down and the windows stop rattling, females verbally attack their asses with vengeance. They rant and rave! Soon their verbally battered butts become known as the biggest *lard asses* in the history of lard asses! At the end of their tirades, the females say they will never wear bikinis again! They find a pair of scissors and cut up their tape measures! A week later the females buy more tape measures and start this crazy process all over again. Talk about personutilties!

As fat cells can see from this presentation, they are in for a *bumpy ride* on female butts! Do not count on anything feeling normal there! Some females will always have *asinine ass afflictions*! Fat cells must persevere! What ever happens, do not feel guilty about your presence in female asses. If fat cells were not there, the pelvic bones would only be covered by muscles, tendons and ligaments. How would you like to sit down on that? Where's the comfort?

With regards to cellulite cells in the buttocks, the underlying fat cells will do everything they can to support them. All fat cells have to work together. Try to find a friend who can be a buddy to you at this site. Hold on tight!

Many female humans spend a great amount of time trying to rid themselves of cellulite cells. Some of them will exercise vigorously. If cellulite cells feel their demise is imminent, they should quickly find a cellulite escape channel. These channels are on all human asses. Fatpocrates designed these centuries ago as safeguards for cellulite cells. Please consult the ass maps in your cellulite cell manuals for safe havens. One such area is the mons pubis. Cellulite cells who flee to this area should remain there until they are summoned to serve elsewhere. Attention cellulite cells! Please ignore any moans or groans coming from the pubic area!

One final note! Ass assignments can be very stressful! If you need psychological help, please let us know! We have a great psychiatrist named Dr. R. U. Nuttee on our staff.

Here's a credo for you: "Cellulite on the ass is never crass!"

The Human Thighs

Thanks to the *femur* bones, the thighs are powerful pillars of strength. There is one femur in each thigh, and they are the biggest and longest bones in the human body. Fat cells strengthen the thighs by insulating the femurs.

Thighs are prime locations for cellulite cells. One may say, cellulite cells are in their element when they are in the thighs. They even have contests to see which cellulite cell is the lumpiest. After they have paraded around, a *pudge judge* picks a winner. It is all in good fun. Fat cells feel this is cellulite cell camaraderie at its best.

As much as cellulite cells enjoy their time in the thighs, they know it is not always fun and games there. BE WARNED! Most humans hate cellulite on their thighs; especially females! Cellulite ridden thighs are prime targets for verbal abuse. Fat cells and cellulite cells have heard humans refer to chunky thighs as *thunder thighs* and *tree trunks*. Not only do thighs receive a lot of flak, but some humans take them for granted. How dare they? If the great sculptor *Fatangelo* had felt that way, he would not have carved the fabulous statue of David. What a loss for the fat cell world. The thighs on that work of art are almost saintly!

Some humans love their thighs and exercise daily. Many of them lift weights and achieve extremely muscular thighs. This makes fat cells feel left out, nevertheless we have to admire those humans. After all, even fat cells have to give credit where credit is due! Besides, sooner or later there is always a chance, albeit a slim one, fat cells may find a home in some of those thighs.

Here is a credo for fat cells and cellulite cells in the thighs: "No matter what their size, all fat cells love the thighs!"

The Human Lower Legs/Calves

Many humans consider the lower legs two of the sexiest parts of the human body. Shapely female legs, which are also called *pins*, *stems* and *gams* receive a lot of attention from male humans. Males' fascination with female legs has a profound effect on both genders. In some cases societal norms are shaped by humans' preoccupation with female legs. When females desire to be accepted, some of them bow to social pressures and wear high heel shoes to make their legs look more attractive. Fat cells think this is a ridiculous standard for female humans. Further education about the discomfort caused by those particular types of shoes will be addressed in the section on the feet.

Attention fat cells! There are some things you need to know before you begin rotations in the lower legs. The back parts of the lower legs are called the calves. The *gastrocnemius muscles* which are essential for the movements in the lower legs reside there. These mean muscles are prime locations for painful spasms called *Charlie horses*. Fat cells in the calves have experienced great pain because of these brutish muscles. They are bullies, and they hate fat cells too! Gastrocnemius muscles are our nemeses! Fortunately, only a few fat cells are required there.

We ask fat cells to be alert when they leave the cell depots to serve rotations in various parts of the human body. For those of you who must serve in the feet, stay in large groups when you travel through the lower legs on your way to the feet.
Please try to avoid the calves. We do not want any fat cells to be battered or bruised by the brutal gastrocnemius muscles.

After the appropriate number of fat cells have located themselves in the feet, the rest of them will protect the front sides of the lower legs. These areas are called the *shins.* Due to humans' physical activities, the shins often collide with hard objects. Ow! Fat cells should expect to be knocked about when this happens. **Be warned**! It is imperative for fat cells who have been bumped to avoid falling into bruised blood vessels. Once fat cells are commingled with dense bruised blood vessels, they may never escape. All compromised fat cells should flee to other areas. They must take care to avoid running smack dab into the gastrocnemius muscles. These menacing muscles could cause more harm to fat cells than the most bloodthirsty blood vessels!

Thanks to their legs, humans engage in all sorts of sporting events. They enjoy playing football, basketball, baseball, volleyball, rugby, soccer, cricket, tennis, table tennis, ice hockey, field hockey and golf. Humans also participate in wrestling, boxing, skiing, fencing and ice skating. The list of activities can go on and on. Fat cells believe the legs can go on and on allowing humans to cover ground, race like the wind, make tracks and dance the night away!

Oh, fat cells forgot to mention. . . *walking*! Some fat cells believe walking allows humans to analyze angst, consider conundrums, decipher dilemmas and ponder problems. In other words, humans clear their minds of damaging debris. Other fat cells believe walking allows humans to get a breath of fresh air, stop and smell the roses, listen to the birds sing and feel the sunshine on their faces. In any event, walking is wonderful!

When fat cells see humans move, they are thrilled. Fat cells realize physical exercise perks up humans' appetites. Their hungry tummies need some nutritious snacks. Bring on the platters full of fruits and vegetables!

Here is a catchy credo: "The lower legs are really grand, thanks to fat cells who help them stand."

The Human Feet

We want to remind all fat cells, the humans struggled to gain a foothold in the world around them. Oftentimes they did not know which way to turn. Humans had to *think on their feet*! In their quest for better lives they walked millions of miles, and fat cells were with them every step of the way. We shudder to think what they would have done without us! Fat cells provided critical fat pad support in the heels, in the balls of the feet and in the toes. Good food and nutrition gave humans stamina. Fat cells gave humans physical support which enabled them to stand for long hours and accomplish a variety of tasks.

Fat cells are proud to have helped the humans who stood on us as they built cathedrals, ships, homes, factories, hospitals, schools and other useful structures for their fellow humans. We are thrilled to have left our footsteps in every one of those creations! However, it was not always an easy road for fat cells! There were some potholes along the way!

Our fat cell forefathers and their heirs would agree, fat cells in the feet suffer the most abuse of any location in the human body! Many fat cells feel real pain when their humans walk. It turns into a *step. . . ouch, step. . . ouch*, situation! Remember, fat cells are bearing untold pounds of pressure in those feet!

Fat cells do not mean to complain but it seems that many humans do not respect their feet. Frankly, we are amazed at the way some humans take their feet for granted. Many humans treat their feet like a couple of stinky stubs. It is as though they want nothing to do with them. How do they think their fat cells feel? We have no avenue of escape from humans' gigantic odiferous feet! Some feet smell like rotten cheese! We wish humans would remember what Lardo Da Fatvinci said:

"The human foot is pretty, and it is a mechanical marvel!"

Fat cells must brace themselves for a rigorous time while in the feet. They will experience walking, running, jumping, dancing and many other activities that end in *ing*! Fat cells hope active humans soak their feet in bath salts when they are finished with those activities!

We must warn fat cells about *stilettos*, which are high heel shoes some females wear. Hello! A stiletto is a dagger! Fat cells feel stabbing pain when feet are crammed into these shoes. The feet are so contorted, fat cells in there look like smashed fish eggs. If they were pressed any closer together, their formation would look like one big blob of fat instead of individual fat cells. This type of physical torture could cause an identity crisis in any fat cell. We protest these types of shoes. If it were up to us, these torture devices would be banned! By the way, fat cells rarely see male humans wearing stiletto shoes!

It is time for fat cells to learn about another important issue; *geriatric feet*! Sadly, many older humans are unable to properly care for their feet. As a result, geriatric feet may look like crusty, scaly appendages. Fat cells may see long hideous toenails that resemble claws! Some humans have gigantic, *big toes* that crowd and grasp the smaller neighbor toes. These scary things are called *hammer toes*! When fat cells see these oddities, they must not scream and run the other way!

The *thinning* of feet fat pads is another condition which affects some older humans. Without proper fat cell cushions on their feet, it is painful for them to walk! Both of these conditions mean older humans need fat cells more than ever! Please do your duty and maintain your proper placement in the geriatric feet.

We realize some fat cells may have suffered psychological damage due to their service in unsightly or smelly feet! If you feel the least bit *psycho*, please visit Dr. R. U. Nuttee!

Please remember this credo: "Thanks to fat cells in their feet, humans accomplish many *feats!*"

Fat Cells'
Lessons, Rules & Credos

1. All fat cells were created to encourage laughter and help perpetuate the human race. We believe the phrase, *the more the merrier*, applies beautifully to us!

2. If God did not want humans to enjoy their food, he would not have created taste buds!

3. Attention all fat cells! Humans live within a physical parameter called *homeostasis*. It means that all bodily systems are functioning normally. If any fat cells refuse to act appropriately, human lives could be in danger. Please behave yourselves! Fat cells who commit grievous errors will be punished!

4. Do not bully your fellow fat cells! We will not tolerate this behavior!

5. When humans eat less, some fat cells shrink down to thinner, *flat cells*. These flat fat cells patiently wait in cell depots until they are needed. When humans eat more food, the flat fat cells are pumped up and come out of cell depots to serve rotations again. All fat cells know it is the rhythm of their lives to be *fluctuating blobs of fat*.

6. The lipids in fat cells come from foods humans eat.

7. Fat cells are made up of lipids (liquid fat), cytoplasm, mitochondria and a nucleus. They are responsible for checking their lipid levels daily with their lipid readers.

8. If you hear a human laugh, give yourself a pat on the back for a job well done!

9. Cellulite cells must present a dimply appearance. If your lipid lining is making you appear too smooth, please go to the squeezing spa where you will be given more dimples.

10. Please strive to maintain your plumpness if a human tries to reshape you with yoga.

11. The *lite* in the word cellulite means cellulite cells shimmer like beacons.

12. It is against the rules for fat cells and cellulite cells to discuss the heinous undergarments known as girdles or body shapers. These latex body chokers were created to torture and torment female cellulite cells.

13. For those fat cells who serve a rotation in the humans feet, bear with us! Yes, we know you are literally bearing the full brunt of the weight (which sometimes feels like a three ton elephant). Hang in there!

14. All fat cells and cellulite cells shall revere the humans!

15. Forget rule #14. Revere is too strong a word! Just try to like humans!

16. Remember, a dimple a day is a cellulite cell's way!

17. Many female humans try to massage away their cellulite with assorted expensive creams. Cellulite cells believe the creams will not work. Please resist all efforts on the humans part to smooth you out.

18. When fat cells are located in the inner thighs, they must

watch out for thighs that rub together. This type of friction can cause tempers to flare among both fat cells and cellulite cells. Please embrace our Cellulite Cell Charm Center credo: "Cellulite cells have class and charm, to one another they do no harm!"

19. Humans refer to their buttocks as their asses. In order to avoid confusion, fat cells will do the same. Humans who have mass amounts of cellulite cells on their asses sit down a lot. The pressure on cellulite cells will feel tremendous. As you are flattened and squashed against one another, hold on tight! You will eventually plump back into your original selves. Here is a sustaining credo: "Cellulite cells will not squirm, it's their duty to stay firm!"

20. Some humans refer to their buttocks as cheeks. The cheeks in the face will always be referred to as the facial cheeks.

21. Fat cells are sublime all the time!

22. If fat cells see their lipids turning dark, they must immediately go to the Lipid Recirculation Chamber where they will receive treatment to restore their pale color.

23. Body shaping panty hose are literally a pain in the ass. Humans who wear them believe their asses will appear smaller. Fat cells know this is not true. Please remember this credo: "Where there's a human ass that's round, cellulite cells abound!"

24. There will be times when you feel your nucleus is a little overbearing, and your brain is a pain. This is a good time to display your charm and recite: "I will not make noise, instead I will show poise!"

25. When a human gets a Charlie horse in their calf, watch out! Since fat cells are above muscle cells, they may be drawn into the fray. Muscle cells are ruthless! Cellulite and fat cells are not allowed to fraternize with them. Hold fast and pray the Charlie horse gallops away! Credo of encouragement: "Fat cells never show a frown, muscle cells can't bring them down!"

26. Do not forget! The mitochondria are the powerhouses of fat cells. Trust their judgment! There may be times when they instruct you to move quickly. Hesitation on your part could cause your demise. Do as they say!

27. If your cellular shell appears leathery, quickly go to the Lipid Recirculation Chamber. You may need an infusion of lipids. Hopefully, we will have some on hand.

28. If fat cells are located in a human's eye, they should try to avoid the tear duct. Otherwise, they may float away when the human cries.

29. If your human begins a sneezing fit, immediately seek shelter! We do not want to lose any fat cells due to flying mucus!

30. All educational materials were created by a committee of your peers. Every effort was made to provide the proper information which all fat cells need for their service to humans.

31. Fat cell anarchy is forbidden! Do it and you'll get dipped!

32. Creativity is wonderful! We encourage fat cells to be creative. However, that does not mean a fat cell can bungee jump off a lymph node or slide down their

human's spinal cord. Behave!

33. If you want to submit a new credo, put it in the credo suggestion box at the Fatistotle Cellulite Cell Charm Center. You will be notified within thirty days if your credo was accepted. Cross your little pudgy fingers!

34. When a fat cell is located in a nutty human, watch out! Their nuttiness may be contagious!

35. Lipid is the nectar of a fat cell's life.

36. Attention cellulite cells! Some of you may be located in humans who resent your presence. Unfortunately, many humans find cellulite cells revolting! Please brace yourselves! Some humans may be in shock when they see cellulite on their bodies. Many of them believe they should never have cellulite. Be warned! They may act maniacal in their efforts to rid themselves of you. These humans might pound on you and call you fat bastards. Vigorous exercise may be used by some of them. This may cause their muscle cells to rise up in revolt. Do not be surprised if they display an instantaneous revulsion for cellulite cells. As far as muscle cells are concerned, cellulite cells are just a bunch of blubbery fat cells. Do not back down! Persevere and take heart! The humans will not be able to exercise all the time. They will spend hours lamenting about what foods to eat. Some of them may consume atrocious items that taste like cardboard. This consumption of questionable food harms not only cellulite cells but anal fat cells as well. Remember, humans have to sleep! As they lay shame and blame upon themselves in their dreams, cellulite cells will have at least 6 to 8 hours before another assault begins. Cellulite cells should know there are times of the month called menstruation when female humans laze about like slugs

bemoaning their fate. During these times, cellulite cells will be safe from an assault. Some of these female humans will gorge on chocolate while they lambaste any and all males who are stupid enough to come near them. Please recite one of our favorite credos: "Cellulite cells are filled with cheer, there is nothing that they fear!"

37. Please remember it is the fat cell's duty to encourage their human to eat. When the opportunity presents itself, go ahead and stimulate their hunger.

38. When fat cells feel giggle bubbles deep inside themselves they are lucky blokes, they should have some fun by telling lots of jokes.

39. We conclude the fat cells' lessons, rules and credos by thanking them for everything they do for humans. All fat cells are expected to obey the rules. The committee realizes some rules are very strict. However, they are necessary to protect the humans. As we said before, fat cells exist to help humans have laughter and longevity.

*   *   *

An introduction to Dr. R. U. Nuttee follows.

Introduction to
Dr. R. U. Nuttee

Dr. R. U. Nuttee is a preeminent psychiatrist who has used time travel for many years to administer to troubled fat cells. Dr. Nuttee earned his bachelor's degree with suma cum loony honors from The Crazoid Institute of Nuttier Learning. He earned his master's degree with magna cum loony honors from Screw Loose University. His M.D. degree was awarded at The Mindbenders Institute of Psychiatric Phenomena.

For those of you who have never met Dr. Nuttee, please do not be afraid of him. He is a charming fat cell who is well schooled in his discipline. Speaking of discipline, Dr. Nuttee is an old fashioned doctor who tries to be fair with everyone. However, we must advise you Dr. Nuttee is not one of those doctors who lets you recline on a sofa and whine about your insignificant problems. He likes to cut through to the heart of the matter. He says what he thinks! Do not try to pull any *bull crap* on Dr. Nuttee. He will administer swift punishment if you do so. Please remember! When all fat cells cooperate with one another, goodwill is felt by all.

We are delighted to let you know that Dr. Nuttee has decided to make his self-evaluation available for fat cell scrutiny. He has also decided to give us a glimpse inside the psychological world of fat cells. Dr. Nuttee accomplished this by publishing a compendium of some of his patients. He did this so other troubled fat cells will come forward when they feel desperate and need guidance.

Dr. Nuttee does not seek to embarrass any of his patients. He feels an open and honest policy will engender trust among fat cells. Dr. Nuttee feels the statement, *we are all in this together* lends a cohesive element to fat cells. Be advised, Dr. Nuttee did not ask permission from his patients since most of them don't realize what the hell is going on anyway! The names have not been changed to protect the guilty!

Dr. Nuttee's
Self-Evaluation

I am just arrogant enough to think that I don't need to be evaluated by another psychiatrist. I agree there are a few slick head shrinkers out there who would love to rip my psyche to shreds but I won't let them! I have heard some negative things they said about me. I know they would love nothing better than for me to be an empty cell casing blowing in the wind.

I am more than my reputation. I am a hardboiled survivor. I am going to do this soul searching in my own brutal yet masterful way. So there! As with most professionals I present one side to the public and keep the other side in a plain brown paper bag. My peculiarities fit nicely in the bag. I merely reach in and pull out whatever is needed at the time. I must say, I've had to replace the bag from time to time.

The time has come for me to confront myself. I feel like my mind is a crystal clear mass of ice filled with air pockets full of knowledge. I have lost track of my soul. Perhaps it vanished like an unwanted thought.

I readily admit I am an indifferent arrogant fat cell. I hate being a callous ass! I have lost my ability to extend empathy to others. I yearn for it to come naturally as it did in my younger years. I had high hopes for fat cell-kind in those days. I charged ahead like a gallant warrior, ready to provide hope and care for any fat cells. I failed to realize hope is a fragile gift which can be crushed by the uncaring acts of others.

I know on the surface, where my reputation is reflected in the sheen of a thin veneer, I have helped thousands. If this is true, why do I feel so sad? As I put one foot in front of the other, I wonder if I am out to help someone else or to further my own indifference.

I ache for a pang of eagerness to seize me. I need to invest myself in the feelings of others and ease their fears. I fear my years of working with the mentally ill have hardened me into a cold block of granite which any sculptor would refuse to carve. There are ribbons of mistakes running through my slab of rock. I long for a clean slate. I have abused the medical slate I was given. It is smeared with lost hope, unmet challenges and self doubt.

I wonder how I would have acted if I'd been a male human? Would I have appreciated the wonder of being a human or would I have taken my life for granted? It pains me to reflect on these unreachable goals. I know I can never be a human. I should envy them but somehow I don't.

Maybe not all is lost for me! Maybe I can have hope again! It bodes well that I am still intrigued by my service to humans. Most humans are walking works of art. Their entire bodies from head to toe are brilliant anatomical machines. I wish humans could see themselves as fat cells do. Humans are like unique snowflakes each with their own individual design.

I say to myself: "Dr. Nuttee, you have done a brilliant job of evaluating yourself. Your service to your fellow fat cells is still vital. It is up to you to give them hope and understanding. You haven't lost your soul! It runs like a ribbon of gold through your block of granite. Stop questioning yourself! Pull your hope out of the paper bag and renew your concern for others. Stay fat and continue!"

Dr. Nuttee's Portrait

Dr. Nuttee's Declaration

I make this declaration
in the way of an explanation.
With regards to fat cells creation
what follows, is my summation!

****

****

****

It took the glory of the Lord
to create such a feisty horde
of fat cells happily racing toward
all humans waiting to be adored
by fat cells eager to come aboard.

Looking at Lunatics

When the fat cells discovered there was going to be a section on insane cells, they asked Dr. Nuttee if they could choose the title. He readily agreed. The choices were:

"Psychos on Parade!"

"A Cavalcade of Crazoids!"

"Maniacs on the Move!"

"Insane Idiots!"

"Suffering Sickos!"

"Nervous Nuts!"

"Looking at Lunatics!"

The winning title "Looking at Lunatics" was chosen by an overwhelming number of fat cells. As you can tell by the title, fat cells really do have a sense of humor. Once again fat cells were willing to be good sports and lend a little laughter to an otherwise serious situation. The following medical cases provided by Dr. Nuttee detail the trials and tribulations which some fat cells have endured.

Dr. R. U. Nuttee's Cases

Dr. R. U. Nuttee: Case # 3
Patient Name: Todd the Turmeric Touter
Gender: Male   Wt. 1 nanogram   Ht. 0.1mm

Todd was a stomach fat cell who became obsessed with turmeric the first time he saw mustard. He said turmeric was the best spice ever and the shade of its yellow was *colorific*. At first I thought he might be afflicted with *chromatopsia* (abnormal color vision). That theory was dismissed after a fat cell guard confirmed the color yellow had indeed come into the stomach. Todd's behavior became worse. The following is an excerpt of some of the things he discussed with me: "Doc, I'm obsessed with turmeric and its wonderful yellow color. I want to change my name to Turmeric. I want to write a turmeric limerick. I want to get a color meter so I can measure the intensity of the color. Doc, why isn't everything yellow? Doc, do you smell that? I smell turmeric! Doc, I want to change my name to Turmeric. Did I tell you that already?"

Evaluation Results: Todd was one sick fat cell. He smelled like turmeric and was an odiferous oddity. My office had to be fumigated to remove the obnoxious odor left by him. When Todd returned for his second visit, he brought a balloon filled with turmeric. The son of a bitch popped it and yellow powder sprayed down upon everything. I wanted to throttle Todd, but the little man on my shoulder called *Ethics* stopped me. I sent this loco lout to the Psycho/Sicko Center.

Final Comments: I recruited some *crazoids* in the Psycho/Sicko Center to help me paint Todd's room yellow. I stacked several empty turmeric cans in a corner of his room. When Todd arrived, he made a beeline towards the cans. His screams of anguish echoed off the walls when he discovered the cans were empty. Todd spends his days reciting unintelligible turmeric limericks to his fellow crazy fat cells.

Todd

Dr. R. U. Nuttee: Case # 5

Patient Name: Angus the Angry Anal Cell
Gender: Male   Wt. 1 nanogram   Ht. 0.1mm

Angus was a fat cell who lived in the anus of a famous accordion player. He loved to hear the accordion and wanted to play one. Angus was promised a transfer to the finger fat pads if he practiced finger exercises. He practiced like a fat cell possessed. Unfortunately, Angus was deemed unfit for finger duty because of his fetid odor. Frankly, he smelled like poop! Angus was furious. His anger flared like a hemorrhoid on fire. He raced up and down the anal canal threatening many of his fellow fat cells with a piece of undigested sausage casing. Some of his comments were: "Doctor Nuttee, I ain't taking the blame for that ass fiasco. Those assholes set me up. They knew a stinky anal fat cell couldn't make it to the top."

Evaluation Results: Angus was red with anger when I first counseled him. For a moment, I lost my composure and almost fled. However, I didn't want to seem like a coward to Beulah the Buxom Beauty who was in the waiting room. She was a hot cellulite cell I really wanted to examine. I took a moment to compose myself. Angus became enraged by my silence and snarled, "What are you afraid of Doc? Haven't you ever seen an angry anal fat cell before? Let's go down to anal hell together! Then you can see why I wanted to leave there!" "No thanks," I said; as two large anal fat cell guards grabbed Angus. The cold hand of terror gripped me when Angus shouted: "Be afraid, Dr. Nuttee. Be very afraid!"

Final Comments: I was afraid! I felt such fear that I leaked lipid oil into my best trousers. Thanks to that sicko, I had to go to the dry cleaners. I hate the smell there! There was only one way to handle this psycho. Lock him up! To placate the angry asshole, we gave him a plastic accordion.

Angus

Dr. R. U. Nuttee: Case # 6

<u>Patient Name</u>: Beulah the Buxom Beauty

Gender: Female   Wt. 1 nanogram   Ht. 0.1mm

Beulah was a beautiful cellulite cell. She was a newcomer to the female breasts. The ancestral breast fat cells made every effort to make Beulah feel welcome. After spending several months in the breasts, Beulah became obsessed with having big boobs. Some other fat cells warned her against such foolish behavior. Beulah didn't care! Because of her naiveté, she begged her fellow fat cells for advice on how to enlarge her boobs. Beulah manipulated and squeezed her own tissue relentlessly while trying to make her boobs bigger. Her actions became more and more erratic. Beulah slowly became mentally unstable. She was brought to me for analysis.

Evaluation Results: Beulah insisted on seeing me once a month. In her mind, I was a medical doctor who could confirm that she did indeed have big breasts. Beulah was one good looking cellulite cell. It was hard to say no to her. Every month I made a dramatic announcement to her about how nice her breasts looked. Beulah acted triumphantly as she said her usual spiel: "I told those bitches around the nipple I had big breasts! They have to believe me now, thanks to your confirmation!" With that statement, she flounced out.

Final Results: I transferred Beulah to the *dewlap* in her female's neck. I figured she needed to get away from the gossipy breast cells who chided her constantly. Beulah was very well received by the neurons who had escaped from the human's brain and took up residence in the dewlap. They spent hours trying to educate her as they lovingly touched her plump cell. Thanks to the neurons, Beulah eventually became one of the smartest fat cells in the body. She was transferred back to the breasts where she actively encourages other fat cells.

Beulah

Dr. R. U. Nuttee: Case # 8

Patient Name: Barney the Blarney Blabber Mouth
Gender: Male   Wt. 1 nanogram   Ht. 0.1mm

Barney blustered into my office like a boisterous beast. The minute Barney sat down in the examination chair he started to blab. He burbled and blabbed like a big buffoon. I was tempted to jump out of the window just to get away from him. The only reason I didn't was because I figured the 20 foot drop wouldn't be good for my health. Barney probably thought he had the gift of gab but what he really had was the gift of blab. He spouted off absurdities like an improperly programmed robot. The other fat cells fled when they saw him coming. I can certainly understand why. Barney was sent to me after he yelled at another fat cell and caused a fight. Here are a few comments he made: "Doc, I like to talk. Words are wonderful, don't you agree? Doc, I love the color green. Why aren't there any green parts in the human body? Why isn't the urine green all of the time instead of only on St. Patrick's Day? Why haven't my winning ways won more friends?"

Evaluation Results: This fat cell was so full of himself he wouldn't even let me speak. I became so frustrated that I resorted to an unusual tactic to shut up the loud mouth. I covered Barney's mouth with green duct tape to quiet his speech. He was so thrilled with the color of the tape, he tried to mumble a thank you. I felt guilty. I gave Barney the roll of tape to play with while I devised a plan for his future.

Final Results: Barney was transferred to the lining of his human's bladder. He blabbed so much, some bladder muscles cells threatened to silence him forever. When Barney apologized to them, he was forgiven. They taught him how to blow bubbles in the bladder. Barney has great joy blowing bubbles on St. Patrick's Day when his human drinks green beer.

Barney

Dr. R. U. Nuttee: Case # 11
<u>Patient Name</u>: Clyde the Clod
Gender: Male   Wt. 1nanogram   Ht. 0.1mm

Clyde was a clod who desired to climb the cellular ladder. He
wanted to have clout. Clyde conspicuously clomped around
and demanded a position with status. He was nicely asked to
refrain from his cloddish behavior, but that request only served
to fuel his efforts. Clyde tried to cajole and coerce his way into
a fat cell guard position. When he was told to stop acting like a
clumsy clod, Clyde became violent and went on a rampage. He
latched onto a varicose vein and swung back and forth shouting
obscenities at other fat cells. Clyde was immediately taken to
the Feces Flow Dipping Vat. After he was released, Clyde
made a conscious decision to continue his cloddish ways. He
was promptly taken to his human's thigh muscle and crammed
into a muscle spasm. Every time the muscle contracted Clyde
was squeezed unmercifully.

Evaluation Results: Clyde was the king of clods.   He was
especially dangerous because of his preconceived agenda. It
was preposterous for Clyde to believe that he could climb the
cellular ladder. His callous behavior caused several fat cells to
seek my counsel. It took years for them to recover.

Final Results: Unfortunately for Clyde, the time he spent in
the muscle spasm turned him into a clumsy clown. Clyde was
committed to the Psycho/Sicko Center where he careens along
the corridors like a drunken fool. Clyde constantly refers to a
ladder that he hopes to climb. A fellow patient took pity upon
him and painted a ladder on the wall in his room. Poor Clyde
tries desperately to climb the ladder. Hundreds of scuff marks
are on the wall from his attempts. Clyde is in a perpetual state
of confusion and mumbles constantly about missing the bottom
rung.

Clyde

Dr. R. U. Nuttee: Case # 15

<u>Patient Name</u>: Delilah the Devious Deceiver

Gender: Female   Wt. 1 nanogram   Ht. 0.1mm

Delilah was devoid of any decent manners. Her morals were in a state of decay. She was intent on being a devious deceiver. Delilah constantly desired attention. At every turn, she devised daring ways to distract her fellow fat cells. When Delilah determined that a testosterone laden female fat cell guard was interested in her, she poured on the charm. The poor fat cell guard didn't have a chance. She followed Delilah around like a moon struck idiot. Delilah decided her boobs were too small. She forced the fat cell guard to inject her with some stolen estrogen. Delilah ended up with three boobs. All of the other fat cells laughed at her and called her *triple titties*. Delilah did not care. She loved the extra attention. Delilah thrust her chest at other fat cells. When the fat cell guard found out, she went ballistic. She decided Delilah wasn't a hot dish after all. She was done with Delilah the devious deceiver.

Evaluation Results: Delilah was a perfect text book example of hormones gone wild. However, medically speaking her hormones were not all to blame. I think she was born an indecent ingrate who turned into a devious deceiver. Delilah's devilish ways had to end. As far as I was concerned she was off to the nuthouse, triple titties and all!

Final Results: There was no denying that Delilah was 100% devious. After I committed her to the Psycho/Sicko Center, Delilah complained to the staff that I demanded a kiss from her. Everyone knows that I am too arrogant to demean myself by kissing such an ingrate. Delilah's lie backfired and I had to make an example of her. Her retribution was swift. Delilah was drained of her extra estrogen and was left a flat chested shell of her former self.

Delilah

Dr. R. U. Nuttee: Case # 17
<u>Patient Name</u>: Emanuel the Emancipator
Gender: Male   Wt. 2.3 nanograms   Ht. 0.2mms

Emanuel was a huge fat cell who used his stature to con everyone into believing he was an eloquent educated emancipator. Emanuel used fake maps to convince his fellow fat cells he knew secret channels for fat cell transport. Emanuel promised to emancipate them from their current locations and relocate them via the secret channels. An anal fat cell took Emanuel down to the anus where several fat cells begged for his help. Emanuel was overcome by fumes and turned to run away. Several anal fat cells followed him in hot pursuit. When other fat cells along the way saw the stampede, they ran too. Emanuel raced to the bladder and hid behind a muscle cell. Several of his followers jumped into the bladder like deranged lemings. Since they couldn't swim, it wasn't long before they were flushed down the commode. Emanuel was found half drowned while clinging to a muscle cell.

Evaluation Results: Emanuel was not an emancipator. He was a con artist extraordinaire; who even tried to con me. Emanuel projected casual elegance as he paraded into my office with his head held high. Emanuel spoke eloquently of emancipation and was oblivious to the tragedy he caused. When I advised him several fat cells had perished due to his irresponsibility, Emanuel pulled off his ascot and attempted to strangle me.

Final Results: No one attempts to strangle me, especially with an ascot made from polyester! I mean really, where was the silk? Emanuel was taken to the Psycho/Sicko Center. His eloquence vanished! Emanuel spends his days emoting to a group of disinterested anal fat cells. Since their minds were blown by methane, they could care less about emancipation!

Emanuel

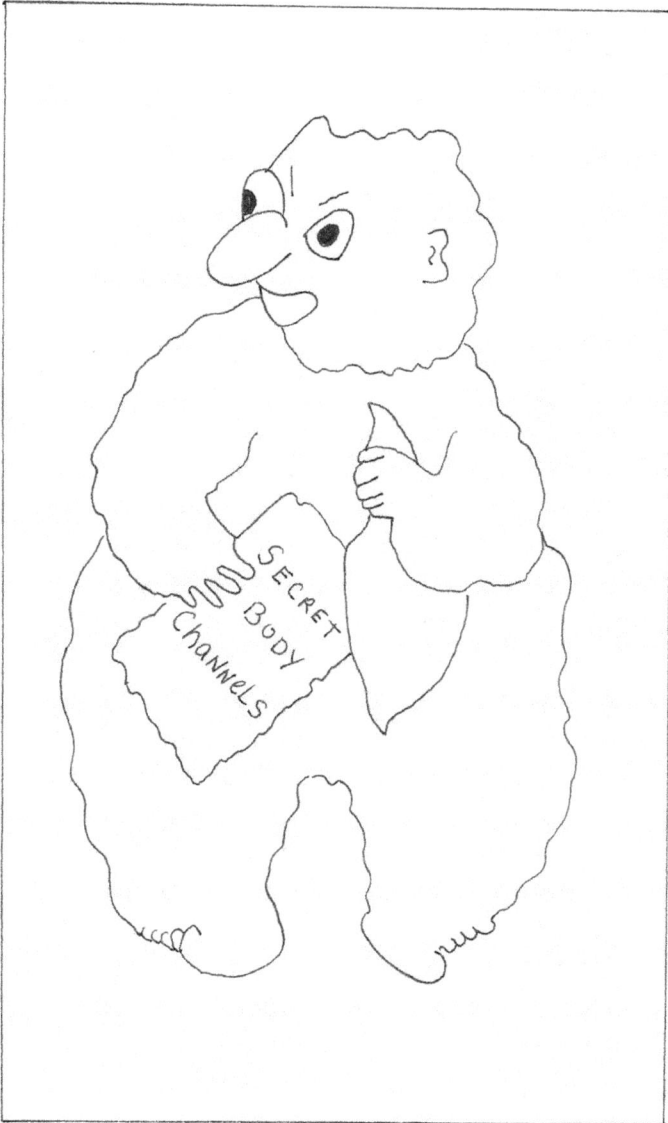

Dr. R. U. Nuttee: Case # 20
Patient Name: Archie the Agitator
Gender: Male   Wt. 2 nanograms   Ht. 0.1mm

Archie loved to travel to hairy areas of the body and provoke the *arrectores pilorum* muscle cells into action. He was delighted by seeing *goose bumps* which resulted when the muscles were stimulated in a certain way. Archie decided to turn his agitating into a game. He began to give names to the locations where goose bumps occurred. Some of his titles were: *alarm in the arm*, *pest in the chest*, and *rub us in the pubis*. The pubis was his favorite spot. Archie jabbed at the arrectores pilorum muscle cells and called them asexual assholes. As they sprang into action he danced around like a lunatic. Archie was caught red handed by fat cell guards who took him to the Feces Flow Dipping Vat. After several dunks, Archie swore he would behave. When some arrectores pilorum muscles cells laughed at him, he began agitating again with a vengeance. Archie was in a state of violent agitation when he was captured. He was promptly dragged to my office!

Evaluation Results: It took me almost two hours to settle this lunatic down. Because of this asinine asshole, I had to reschedule my second session with Beulah the Buxom. I was furious! Archie knew he shouldn't provoke the arrectores pilorum cells. Archie wanted a fast cheap thrill and that's how he got it. There would be no more goose bumps for Archie!

Final Results: As a special favor to me, Archie was taken to the Psycho/Sicko Center by two arrectores pilorum muscle cells. Those muscle cells told Archie they were going to make some goose bumps in the pubis. He went beserk and escaped. Archie was heard screaming and yelling as he raced toward the pubis. Archie succumbed to lipid dehydration and met his demise while trapped in some dense pubic hairs.

Archie

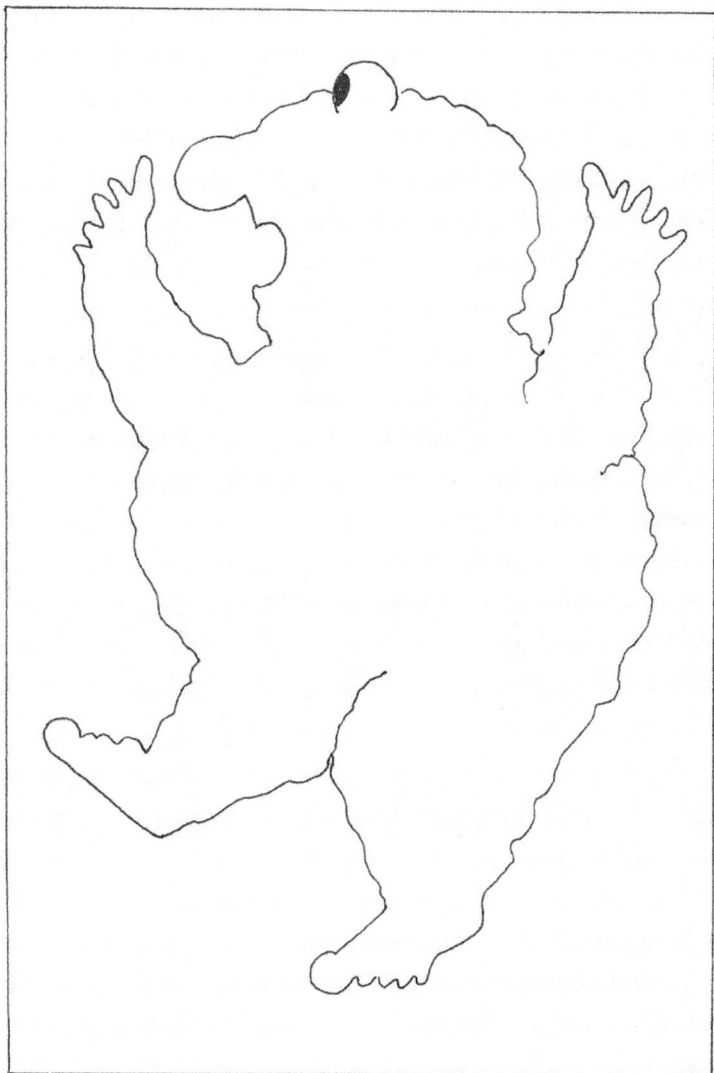

105

Dr. R. U. Nuttee: Case # 21
<u>Patient Name</u>: Jonah the Jovial Whale
Gender: Male   Wt. 1 nanogram   Ht. 0.1mm

Jonah started out his life as a congenial anal fat cell. Jonah had a bubbly personality and was welcome wherever he went. For reasons unknown, Jonah slowly morphed into a grotesque whale shape. His transition was so gradual many of his fellow fat cells didn't realize what was happening. Jonah felt different, but he continued to be his jovial self. Everyone became suspicious when bubbles frothed from his mouth. An examination revealed Jonah had been contaminated by his human eating too much mercury tainted fish. Some other fat cells avoided him because he smelled fishy and emited an eerie orange glow. The one cell who remained loyal to Jonah was Ernest the Eyeball. Ernest had suffered a similar fate involving his eyes due to contamination. Jonah asked to see me so he could obtain some advice.

Evaluation Results: This was one whale of a fish tale! It would have been hilarious if it weren't so serious. When are humans going to clean up things? I don't care to expostulate very often; however, if the humans can fly to the moon, why can't they protect the oceans? Anyway, Jonah was not insane just badly damaged. He and Ernest were nice fat cells! No one should judge them by their appearances. Jonah and Ernest deserve appreciation for their kindness!

Final Results: As a doctor I see all kinds of maladies. I have to steel myself like a fat cell made of marble to give my patients hope for the future. If they saw a weakness in me, it could become theirs. No fat cells have touched me more deeply than Jonah and Ernest! They were appointed goodwill ambassadors. Thanks to them, many fat cells received hope and encouragement.

Ernest & Jonah

Dr. R. U. Nuttee: Case # 24
<u>Patient Name</u>: Queenie the Quibbler
Gender: Female   Wt. 1 nanogram   Ht. 0.1mm

There was no triviality to small for Queenie to quibble over.
She argued from morning to night. In order to become more
proficient at quibbling, Queenie made lists of trivial items. She
wanted to be the quickest quibbler in the whole fat cell block.
Queenie begged other fat cells to quibble with her. She was an
argumentative, quarrelsome fussbudget who drove the other fat
cells nuts. They devised a plan to thwart her. Some of the fat
cells altered Queenie's lists so items reflected the opposite of
what they meant. A fat cell guard challenged her to a quibbling
contest. Queenie readily accepted and quoted trivia. Each
statement she made was wrong. Queenie checked her lists and
gasped at the horrendous mistakes she had made. A queasy
feeling came over her. To quell her dismay, Queenie hid behind
a benign tumor. The fat cell guard coaxed her out of hiding and
told her to schedule a visit with Dr. R. U. Nuttee.

Evaluation Results: Having been through countless years of
learning, including medical school, I knew a thing or two about
extraneous trivia. I wondered why anyone would bother with
it. It is true that facts can be fun but when they become an
obsession, reality takes a hike. I had to get Queenie back on
track. Queenie knew she had a problem and requested to go to
the Psycho/Sicko Center. She was given permission to compile
trivia while at the Center.

Final Results: In all actuality Queenie was a harmless,
eccentric know it all. I've seen many fat cells worse than her.
Queenie was a nice diversion for some of the lunatics in the
center. They thought she was a real queen. They gave Queenie
a plastic tiara and a purple crushed velvet robe. She held court
daily and regaled her subjects with bits of trivia.

Queenie

Dr. R. U. Nuttee: Case # 27
<u>Patient Name</u>: Ned the Necrotic Tissue Seeker
Gender: Male   Wt. 1 nanogram   Ht. 0.1mm

Ned had a neurosis about necroses. He was a neurotic nerd
who gave everyone the heebeejeebies because of his obsession
with necrotic tissue. Ned made nightly forays all over his
human's body searching for injured flesh. He howled insanely
whenever any damaged tissue was found. Ned's eyes took on a
wild glint when he prodded areas that were not even diseased.
Some of the other fat cells thought Ned was purposely injuring
normal tissue. Due to his misguided judgment, Ned thought a
wart was necrotic. The wart's virus attached itself to Ned and
began to overtake him. He ran screaming to the stomach
hoping the acid there would loosen the virus. Ned's plan
worked but his outer shell peeled horribly. He looked like a
piece of necrotic tissue himself. Ned was sent to me as a result
of his stupidity.

Evaluation Results: I emphatically state: "Ned gave me the
creeps!" It is not normal for fat cells to touch necrotic tissue.
Where did this throw back from ancient times come from?
Talk about recessive genes! His human's gene pool had some
nasty crap floating in it! I didn't go to med school for this!
Fatpocratic oath or not, Ned was too much for me to stomach.
I sent him to the Psycho/Sicko center within the hour.

Final Results: As soon as Ned arrived at the center, he began
snooping around. The staff was aware of his neurosis.
Fortunately, none of the other patients had scabs or injuries. I
decided to limit Ned's time with other fat cells in case he tried
to physically damage them. In order to keep Ned occupied, we
gave him a bucket of old epithelium (skin) cells. I told him to
make collages with them. Ned eventually became famous for
being the first fat cell to become a *modern artist*.

Ned

Dr. R. U. Nuttee: Case # 28
Patient Names: Flotsam & Jetsam
Gender: Males   Wt. 1 nanogram   Ht. 0.1mm

Flotsam and Jetsam were aptly named. They looked like they
had been floating in the ocean for years. Their cells were an
ugly olive green color that appeared to be glazed with a shade
of orange. We overlooked their strange appearance and
accepted them as fat cells. Flotsam and Jetsam worked hard to
make friends. It was all a ruse. One night they crept up to their
human's head and hid in between the skin and the skull. They
didn't know a fat cell guard had followed them. He heard them
communicate with an alien planet. The fat cell guard nearly
lost his lipids on the spot from what he heard. He made a quick
exit. The alien spies were trying to ascertain whether humans
were worth a takeover. Flotsam and Jetsam relayed this
message to their mother ship: "The humans are all nuts down
here, don't bother coming down!"

Evaluation Results: I knew these gangrenous looking creeps
were trouble the moment I saw them. However, I still had to
check out the fat cell guard's story. He acted shifty and was
turning green. Alarm bells rang in my mind when I realized the
aliens had taken him over. I slapped handcuffs on the fat cell
guard and locked him to a heavy iron door. Four, burly muscle
cells helped me catch Flotsam and Jetsam. We hauled the three
aliens down to the anus. Within a minute, they were blown to
kingdom come by a blast of flatulence.

Final Results: I wasn't about to change the Psycho/Sicko
Center into the Psycho/Sicko UFO Center. Those alien
assholes had to be disposed of immediately. If my methods
seemed harsh to some, too bad! I was not taking any chances
with the safety of my humans and their fat cells. Aliens
beware! Your demise is just a fart away!

Flotsam & Jetsam

Dr. R. U. Nuttee: Case # 30
Patient Name: Quake the Quaker
Gender: Male   Wt. 1 nanogram   Ht. 0.1mm

Quake was an abdominal fat cell who had the misfortune of living in a human who went through an earthquake. He was all shook up! Quake was in constant fear of another earthquake. He obsessed about tremors, fault lines, and tectonic plates. When a fat cell guard showed him a seismogram from a seismograph instrument, Quake begged for his own seismograph. When his request was refused, he flipped out and couldn't stop quaking. The situation became worse when Quake's human skipped a meal and hunger pangs rumbled throughout his abdomen. Quake was sure it was another earthquake. He didn't believe it was hunger pangs. Many fat cells tried to help him quell his quakes, but nothing worked. Quake was in a desperate state when he was brought to me.

Evaluation Results: Poor Quake was shuddering and trembling violently when I first met him. His fear was all in his mind. I just wanted to shake the living daylights out of Quake to give him something to really shake about! It would have been fun to put him in a salt shaker! Not really! I tried to hypnotize Quake but it didn't work. He claimed I made him dizzy and caused his brain to quiver. I was just about ready to make Quake's brain quiver with a *fatbotomy*!

Final Results: Thankfully, the thought of a fatbotomy was fleeting. I immediately ruled out that idea since I had never performed one! I had to protect my reputation, which was and is: *too keep all the marbles in all the fat cell brains*! Quake was not insane, nor was he capable of hurting anyone. After careful consideration, I put Quake in the diaphragm where he picked up good vibrations and kept time with his human's breathing.

Quake

Dr. R. U. Nuttee: Case # 33
Patient Name: George I & George II the Goofballs
Gender: Males   Wt. 1 nanogram   Ht. 0.1mm

George I and George II were very limber blobs of blubber.
They were roly-poly twin fat cells who excelled at goofing off.
The two fat cells lived in the back of a professional bowler.
They saw balls flying all day long. George I said to George II,
"I bet I can make myself into a ball shape faster than you can."
As it often happens between siblings, the race was on. In a
matter of moments the two Georges had transformed into
goofballs. They were soon rolling and bouncing off the walls.
The other fat cells thought the Georges were hilarious.
Laughter echoed throughout the area! However, things became
tense when the goofballs pretended the other fat cells were
bowling pins and tried to knock them down. The situation
became worse when the Georges accidentally knocked over a
fat cell guard. The fat cells who witnessed it said the fat cell
guard growled like a dragon when he stood up. The Georges
ran screaming from the scene. The fat cell guard followed in
hot pursuit shouting that he would kill both of them.

Evaluation Results: I laughed until my sides hurt when I
heard this story. There is nothing better than a good belly
laugh! I wish I could have seen the fat cell guard's face. He
must have looked hilarious! Anyway, the only injury the guard
suffered was a bruised ego. I sent him to the human's pubis
where there would be lots of distraction. It was obvious
George I and George II were not insane, just nuts!

Final Results: It would be a cold day in hell before I would do
anything to punish George I and II. Thanks to them I had the
best laugh ever. The Georges were sent to the funny bone area
where they rolled around to their hearts content.   They proved
that laughter is the best medicine!

George I & George II

Dr. R. U. Nuttee: Case # 35
<u>Patient Name</u>: Knute the Knucklehead
Gender: Male   Wt. 1 nanogram   Ht.0.1mm

Knute was an abdominal cellulite cell who narrowly escaped a liposuction operation. Unfortunately, the top of his head was damaged during his escape. His head was turned into huge knobby knobs. Knute's noggin looked like a set of brass knuckles. He became the butt of jokes as the other fat cells knocked his noggin. Knute didn't care because he had developed a fear of noise called *acousticophobia.* He didn't have time to worry about frivolous jokes. Knute walked around warily nodding his head from side to side listening for a liposuction tube. On the day his human used a brand new electric razor, Knute nearly lost it. He screamed bloody murder thinking the liposuction tube was back and after him again. Knute almost caused a cellulite cell collapse. Fortunately, a fat cell guard was near and grabbed Knute before he had a chance to wreak havoc. Knute screamed like a maniac when the fat cell guard brought him to see me.

Evaluation Results: There is not much you can say to a fat cell who has seen his family and friends sucked down a liposuction tube. If it had happened to me, I would be scared shitless too! I knew that music worked wonders with mental patients; I put on Fatbert's Serenade. It helped to calm us down. When Knute requested it again, I felt confident he would benefit from music therapy.

Final Results: Knute was placed in the Psycho/Sicko Center where he was given music therapy. We used a variety of classical music. Knute would have none of it. He screamed for Fatbert's Serenade. When Knute listened to Fatbert's music, his health greatly improved. As for me, I give thanks for the brilliant fat cell composer Fatbert.

Knute

Dr. R. U. Nuttee: Case # 38

Patient Name: Enus the Enunciator
Gender: Male   Wt. l nanogram   Ht. 0.lmm

Enus was an unusual fat cell with a huge mouth and a proclivity for speech making. He loved words and was a motor mouth with an engine that would not shut off. In addition he claimed to have an addiction to lip puckering. Enus moved his lips around so much his mouth looked like an anus turned inside out. That earned him the nasty nickname of Enus the Anus! Thankfully, a few fat cells still called him Enus the Enunciator. He loved to enunciate so much he chased other fat cells down and challenged them to out do him. Most fat cells refused which made Enus mad. Some fat cells called him an eccentric egomaniac and threatened him with bodily harm. Enus ran towards the offenders and told them about the importance of enunciation. Most of those fat cells laughed at him. Enus became sad and said, "I will never enunciate again! Now I know how Fat Gogh felt when he said: 'I am Fat Gogh, why can't the other fat cells accept me for who I am?'"

Evaluation Results: Damn that beats all! Enus quoted my favorite artist so now I felt as though I had to like him as well as help him. I hate it when fat cells play mind games with me and win! However, I too have a proclivity for public speaking. Enus wasn't insane so I decided to give him the benefit of the doubt. After all, anyone who loves words cannot be all bad!

Final Results: I didn't admit it to anyone else, but Enus and I were actually kindred spirits. I love to enunciate as much as he does. Enus is the only patient I have ever allowed to see my collection of dictionaries. His mouth ran a mile a minute as he raved about them. Since Enus and I both love words, we have a private enunciating competition once a month.

Enus

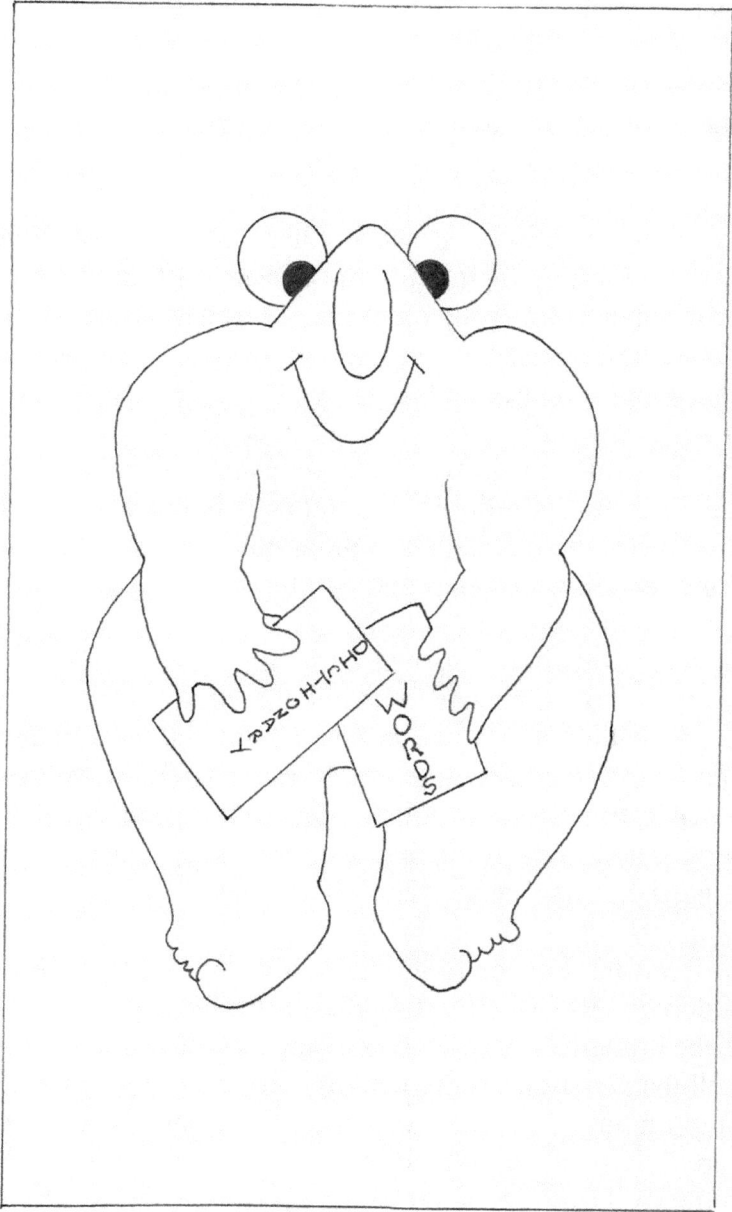

Dr. R. U. Nuttee: Case # 39
Patient Name: Xirena the Seductive Siren
Gender: Female   Wt. 1 nanogram   Ht. 0.1mm

Xirena was a beautiful ancestral breast fat cell. She had the unique distinction of living in the huge breasts of a famous movie star. As it happens with fat cell duty, sometimes only a fine line separates reality from make believe. In Xirena's case, make believe took over. It was not her fault. Xirena's human made several romantic movies and during her time off she was under the sheets doing the real thing. Xirena overheard the movie star talk about love, sex and orgasms. Xirena had wild dreams about romance and imagined herself as a seductive siren who was waiting for her lover to come. Her sanity seemed to slowly drift away as though she were in a sea of sexuality. Xirena's fellow breast fat cells blamed the movie star and threatened to stage a cellular collapse. A quick thinking fat cell guard alerted me to the dire situation.

Evaluation Results: This was a true physical emergency. I had to travel to the breasts to handle this predicament. Boy, when I saw the size of those boobs, I wanted to be a male human! Anyway, that's another fantasy! Xirena wasn't the only one in trouble. A cellular collapse could cause plastic surgery. Thousands of fat cells would be lost. Once I convinced Xirena's supporters of that, they backed off.

Final Results: For the first time in my career, I felt completely bewildered. How was I to tell a beautiful fat cell that she could never be human? I used a clinical approach to explain about the cellular functions in the human body. I convinced Xirena of her importance. I quoted Fatspeare: "Life has made you who you are!" Xirena understood and became a member of the Cellulite Cell Calming and Coping Council where she helps other fat cells to this day.

Xirena

Dr. R. U. Nuttee: Case # 40

<u>Patient Name</u>: Kelcie the Kleptomaniac
Gender: Female   Wt. 1 nanogram   Ht. 0.1mm

Kelcie was a kooky klutz who had a nasty habit of stealing from other fat cells. She was also a cute imp who was hard to resist. No one knows when Kelcie's kleptomania started. However, the stolen items were usually returned the next day. Most fat cells considered Kelcie a harmless kook. Their feelings changed when some of their important lipid reader devices went missing. The readers were an absolute medical necessity. The fat cells were furious! One of them threatened to kick Kelcie in her keister! She claimed innocence. A crowd of angry fat cells stormed Kelcie's area to look for the missing readers. They didn't find any. Delilah, choked out this comment: "I saw the lipid readers here this morning!" A fat cell guard had recognized Delilah the Devious Deceiver and removed the planted evidence. Delilah's proclamation proved her guilt. She was dipped in the Feces Flow Dipping Vat and thrown back into the Psycho/Sicko Center.

Evaluation Results: I can't believe this happened to Kelcie. What were those violent vigilantes thinking? All the offenders were shipped down to the human's gout ridden big toe where they suffered from the shooting pain caused by the gout. I found out how Delilah skipped out of the loony bin. The fat cell who freed her was placed in a varicose vein behind the human's knee! Delilah is now in solitary confinement.

Final Results: Leave it to a sicko to cause trouble for a harmless klepto. After all, Kelcie was innocent! She didn't even realize what she did was wrong. Since Kelcie was imbued with a certain *joie de vivre*, I suggested she become a talent scout leader. Thanks to Kelcie the fat cells have fun performing in skits and musicals.

Kelcie

Dr. R. U. Nuttee: Case # 41
Patient Name: Henry the Hypochondriac
Gender: Male   Wt. 1 nanogram   Ht. 0.1mm

Henry was a hopeless fat cell who was unwittingly sucked into the abyss of his human's hypochondria. He was stuck in the neck of a male human who was beyond bonkers. His human was a hissing hysterical fool who claimed he was afflicted with every ailment known to humankind. Poor Henry was influenced by every word his crazy human said. Henry hallucinated about scabies, rabies, leprosy and other diseases. Paranoia permeated every move he made. Henry claimed that swirling masses of bacteria were floating around him in an attempt to penetrate his cell wall. When other fat cells approached Henry, he screamed they were trying to infect him with botulism bacillus. The situation came to an ugly head when Henry accused a fat cell guard of causing a gigantic carbuncle to appear on his ass. Needless to say, the fat cell guard brought hysterical, psychotic Henry to see me.

Evaluation Results: Henry looked so helpless when he came into my office, I just had to give him a hug. HUGE MISTAKE! Henry screamed in terror and accused me of infecting him with gonococcus germs. There's nothing worse than a fat cell who's a germaphobe. If this crap got out, I'd end up with more patients than I could count! If Henry caused me too much trouble, I'd show him a germ he'd never forget. I was going to have to handle this twerp delicately. Not!

Final Results: Henry refused to enter the Psycho/Sicko Center front door so I jerked the little jerk into the building. To calm Henry down I promised him a position as the chief germ exterminator of the Center. He was thrilled at the chance to kill germs. Henry sterilizes the facility daily. He happily eliminates germs using a wide assortment of toxic germicides.

Henry

Dr. R. U. Nuttee: Case # 42
Patient Name: Idola the Identifier
Gender: Female   Wt. 1 nanogram   Ht. 0.1mm

Idola was an energetic fat cell guard who lived in the fatty
abdomen of a female research scientist. The fat cells Idola
guarded were lazy slobs. They resented her energy and called
Idola names such as *Idumba* and *Idiotola*. She acted indifferent
to the name calling and took an interest in medical issues which
her human discussed. Idola took an impromptu trip around her
human's body. She identified the body parts her human
mentioned in a lecture which started with the letter I. In the
heart muscles Idola found the *intercalcated discs* which help to
connect muscle cells together. She traveled back to the
abdomen to see the *ileocecal valve* that separates the small and
large intestine. In the pancreas Idola saw the magnificent *islets
of langerhans* that secrete insulin and glucagon. After that, she
was off to the mouth where the *isthmus of fauces* opens into the
throat. When Idola returned to her location, she was accused of
shirking her duties. Idola came to see me for advice.

Evaluation Results: First of all, I loved this fat cell! Idola's
keen interest in medical science proved she was a comrade in
arms. I know the other fat cells consider those of us who are
interested in medical science strange birds. So what! Let's not
forget the old axiom: "Birds of a feather stick together!" I
wasn't about to let Idola fly away. She was a sexy chick in a
sporty sort of way.

Final Results: Hey, this Doctor has a right to have a little fun!
Idola and I spent several hours discussing fat cell medicine. I
was so impressed with Idola's knowledge that I gave her a job
in my lab. Idola was a quick study! So far she's identified
almost all of my body parts. . . and Idola has done a great job!

Idola

Dr. R. U. Nuttee: Case # 44
<u>Patient Name</u>: Zig and Zag the Zincifiers
Gender: Males   Wt. 1 nanogram   Ht. 0.1mm

From the moment Zig and Zag came out of the fat cell depot, these two crazy fat cells zipped about like miniature flashes of lightning. Fortunately, a zinging sound was made as they raced around. When the other fat cells heard it, they moved aside. Zig and Zag were very witty. Wonderful zingers were flung by them as they zigged and zagged. On one of their trips they came across a wet undigested zinc tablet. After that, something naughty happened! Zig and Zag grabbed a couple of brushes and proclaimed they were going to *zincify* everything. Before anyone could stop him, Zig rudely painted zinc on some of his fellow fat cells. As he raced away Zig shouted *zincking* was fun. In the meantime Zag attempted to coat a fat cell guard with some zinc. The fat cell guard shouted their zincking days were over! Consequently, Zig and Zag were coated with something smellier than zinc when they were dunked in the Feces Flow Dipping Vat.

Evaluation Results: Spontaneity can be a great asset for fat cells, but Zig and Zag were just too damn spontaneous! If they had taken the time to consider the ramifications of their actions, Zig and Zag wouldn't have been dunked in poop! They had to be taught a lesson. It doesn't pay to act like idiotic crazoids all the time!

Final Results: My fellow medical experts may have said Zig and Zag were victims of a disorder of their respective Ids. Whatever! I think spontaneity is special. However, it is not acceptable when it causes harm to other fat cells. Zig and Zag were given etiquette lessons at the Fatistotle Cellulite Cell Charm Center. They confine their zigging and zagging to a zip line in my extra laboratory.

Dr. R. U. Nuttee: Case # 45

<u>Patient Name</u>: Nixie the Nymphomaniac
Gender: Female   Wt. 1 nanogram   Ht. 0.1mm

Nixie started her life as a nice innocent cellulite cell. She lived
in the pubis of one of the biggest sluts in human history. Never
in her wildest dreams did Nixie believe she would behave in a
sexual manner. Nixie didn't know what she was hearing when
her female uttered grunts of sexual ecstasy. Nixie shyly
approached a fat cell guard and asked about the sounds. The
guard gave her a sly look and said, "Why that's sex honey!
You know fornication!" Nixie blushed and asked, "Do you
mean human reproductive activity?" The fat cell guard roared
with laughter and said, "Oh yes, but this human can't seem to
get it right, so she keeps on trying over and over!" Nixie began
to obsess about sex. She even repeated many of the sexual
statements she overheard. Nixie pretended to be a femme
fatale who needed a stud. When she claimed to be a
nymphomaniac, Nixie was brought to see me.

Evaluation Results: Nixie was no more a *nympho* than I was
a *buffo* muscle cell! Damn, the humans! Don't those over
sexed crazoids think of anything but sex, sex and more sex?
All that free love didn't seem to get them anywhere! As a
psychiatrist I have wondered about human sexual activity but it
sounds too messy for me. I'd rather eat and laugh! Okay, a
little benign touching never hurt anyone. In regards to Nixie, I
couldn't have a pseudo nympho in the Psycho/Sicko Center.
Gawkers would come from all over just to stare at her!

Final Results: I convinced Nixie that she was under a
hormonal hex, *sex spell*! Nixie was relieved to know she
wasn't a nymphomaniac. I put her in the Fatistotle Cellulite
Cell Charm Center where she teaches manners to rowdy fat
cells.

Nixie

Dr. R. U. Nuttee: Case # 46
Patient Name: Flavius the Flat Footed Flubber
Gender: Male   Wt. 2 nanograms   Ht. 0.2mms

Flavius was a big, bulky fat cell who suffered from low self esteem due to his huge flat feet. Flavius constantly tripped over his own feet and flubbed up most tasks he undertook. Flavius was bullied by other fat cells who called him *Flavius the Flubber made of Blubber*! After that, Flavius became so self conscious he refused to do anything for fear of fumbling any job given to him. A fat cell guard took pity upon him and suggested Flavius may become more graceful if he learned ballet. Flavius thought the advice was meant as a mean joke and flipped out. He crashed into the fat cell guard and knocked over a lipid refill dispenser. Oil spilled out everywhere. As Flavius raced away he slipped and slid into a hair follicle. He was found entangled in a mass of hair. Fortunately for Flavius, the fat cell guard was receptive to helping fat cells who had been bullied. The fat cell guard made a wise decision to immediately bring Flavius to see me.

Evaluation Results: I praised the fat cell guard and thanked him for bringing Flavius straight to me. Poor Flavius needed counseling. I wondered why there was so much bullying among fat cells? Didn't any of them read fat cell rule #4? I wanted to cram our anti-bullying rule down all their throats! If the bullying didn't stop, they would all end up at the Feces Flow Dipping Vat, and we would run out of poop! What a load of crap! I didn't want to run out of the stuff.

Final Results: Flavius was just a big teddy bear. He wouldn't harm a microbe. When Flavius heard that humongous human football players took ballet, he tried it! Flavius turned into a graceful athlete. He works in the Fatistotle Cellulite Cell Curriculum Center teaching fat cells to be kind to one another.

Flavius

Dr. R. U. Nuttee: Case # 50
<u>Patient Name</u>: Diana the Ding-a-Ling,
Gender: Female   Wt. 1 nanogram   Ht. 0.1mm

Everyone loves the musical sound of bells. In Diana's case, the
love became an obsession as a result of spending years in the
earlobe of an eccentric elderly female human. She wore
Christmas bell earrings all year long. Diana's human was
ignored by her relatives so she spent her days listening to
musical *objets d'art*. The music was a wonderful part of
Diana's life. All was well until she was transferred to her
human's breast. Diana was confused because the only sounds
she heard were the voices of other fat cells. When Diana asked
about the bells, a fat cell snarled, "Listen girlie you were
brought down here to help lift up this old hag's titties. Her
boobs are sagging so badly, they're about to hit the floor!"
Diana was aghast! "You can't say that! Our human is a sweet
gentle lady," said Diana. The fat cell snarled, "You're a
delusional ding-a-ling." After that, Diana came to see me.

Evaluation Results: Bells are divine and so is Diana.
I admire her for standing up to that crass fat cell. Diana knows
older humans deserve respect! I wish everyone else felt that
way. The elderly possess wisdom that could benefit all of us.
Fatophocles said it best: "As a person grows older they gain
more wisdom."

Final Results: I will not tolerate rude, nasty fat cells snarling
snide comments at innocent fat cells like Diana. I sent the
offender down to the human's anus where she is crammed up
against a hemorrhoid. Diana is a dreamer who loves the sound
of bells. She and I instituted a hand bell class at the Fatistotle
Cellulite Cell Charm Center. Diana's group became a
successful hand bell choir. To the delight of all fat cells, bell
ringing festivals are held every month.

Diana

Dr. R. U. Nuttee: Case # 52
<u>Patient Name</u>: Gunther the Goon
Gender: Male   Wt. 2.5 nanograms   Ht. 0.2mms

Gunther was a gargantuan goon. He was also a fat cell guard who went AWOL. Of all the goons in the world, Gunther was the gooniest. He spent most of his time tracking down goo and gunk. Many believe Gunther suffered brain damage when he was gouged in the head by a stab from an acupuncture needle. That certainly would have made any fat cell cuckoo! Gunther reportedly grabbed gunk such as pus and hid it. He was also seen racing away with some spider veins ripped from his human's nose. His fellow fat cells complained Gunther was getting *goonier* by the minute! Somehow, he got hold of some urine and sprayed it on another fat cell guard. The victim of the assault yelled so loudly that a group of fat cell guards rushed to help. It took three of them to capture Gunther and take him to the Feces Flow Dipping Vat. After the poop was removed from him, he was brought to me.

Evaluation Results: I could still smell poop on this gross goon when he was dragged into my office. I made the fat cell guards take Gunther to the lab and swab him down with alcohol. I put a dab of cologne under my nose to ward off any lingering odor from the gunky goon. The question of the day was, why wasn't I informed when Gunther's brain was pierced by a needle? Incident's such as this made me wonder why I even became a doctor! It was time for me to chew out some fat cells, and I was ready!

Final Results: It felt good to blast the irresponsible fat cell guards who failed to inform me about Gunther. Unfortunately, I couldn't do much for him. Gunther was thrilled to be transferred to his human's enlarged prostate where he plays with a variety of cellular gunk and goo.

Gunther

Dr. R. U. Nuttee: Case # 54
Patient Name: Xavier the Exciter
Gender: Male   Wt. 0.5 nanogram   Ht. 0. 1mm

Xavier was an affable fat cell who lived comfortably in his human's chest. Unfortunately, Xavier suffered brain damage when an x-ray machine malfunctioned during a routine scan. He was bombarded with excessive radiation. Xavier turned into a glowing excitable freak. Sizzling sparks flew out of him as he jumped around and exclaimed to be a, "God of Lightning!" After that, many other fat cells excluded Xavier from their activities. As he became more desperate, his insane behavior intensified! Xavier ran erratically from one location to another screaming his cell was aflame. That rant caused his total exclusion from other fat cells. Xavier became furious and claimed he needed some of his exterior shell excised for examination. When he tried to con another fat cell into scraping off part of his outer shell, Xavier's shenanigans were brought to a halt. A fat cell guard wrapped Xavier in a lead shield and brought him to me.

Evaluation Results: Thank goodness for the quick thinking fat cell guard's use of the lead shield. I wasn't about to become contaminated by radiation and end up bopping around like a brain dead idiot. How can an x-ray be routine? You either suspect a problem or you don't. Humans would worry less about their health if they walked more. Even Fatpocrates knew this thousands of years ago when he said: "All humans should take a walk, it medicates well!"

Final Results: Miraculously, Xavier was the only fat cell injured in that tragic accident. It took months for him to stop sizzling like bacon. His health gradually improved. Since Xavier's injury, his interest in lightning increased. I put him in his human's eyes so he can watch the weather forecasts.

Xavier

Dr. R. U. Nuttee: Case # 56
<u>Patient Name</u>: Zombor the Zombie
Gender: Male   Wt. 3 nanograms   Ht. 0.2mms

Zombor, which is Hungarian for buffalo, was a huge, hulking
ass fat cell. Since he looked like a buffalo, Zombor was aptly
named. He wasn't shaggy or furry but two horned knobs on his
gigantic head sealed Zombor's fate. The curse continued with
his inarticulate grunt like speech which none of the other fat
cells understood. Zombor couldn't contain his frustration so he
often stamped his feet and bellowed at other fat cells. The fat
cell guards were fed up with Zombor. One of them who had
studied *zombiism* pretended to *zombify* Zombor. The fat cell
guard figured the spell might trick him into a more placid state
of being. He fed Zombor part of an old crushed up muscle
relaxant tablet which was previously stolen from the human's
esophagus. The fat cell guard finished with a flourish of
mumbo jumbo as he whispered to Zombor: "You are now a
zombie!" Although he felt dazed, Zombor was furious to have
been a victim of such evil trickery. He raced up his human's
back and accidentally triggered a muscle spasm near the spine.
Zombor became frantic and sought refuge with me.

Evaluation Results: I am as guilty as the next fat cell when it
comes to judging another fat cell by its cover. I suppose it is
only fat cell nature, but when will we learn to accept others for
who they are? Of course Zombor was frustrated! He felt all
alone in a sea of normal fat cells. I was determined to help
him.

Final Results: I reassured Zombor that the muscle relaxant
pill did not harm him. Zombor took speech therapy so he could
speak with clarity to the other fat cells. Zombor became a
storyteller at the Fatistotle Cellulite Cell Charm Center where
everyone praised his folktales about Hungary.

Zombor

Dr. R. U. Nuttee: Case # 58
<u>Patient Name</u>: Quinn the Quipster
Gender: Male   Wt. 1 nanogram   Ht. 0.1mm

Quinn was the quickest quipster who was ever known to the fat cell world. He was a small neck fat cell with a huge mouth. Quinn learned the art of quipping from his human who was a speech writer for a semi-literate political candidate. The speech writer was having a ball creating quips to cover the candidate's lies. Quinn learned a lot and began to imagine himself as a candidate. He perfected his smile and increased his quipping. Quinn announced he wanted to be president of the fat cells. He quipped, "I'm Quinn, just watch me win!" Some fat cells mocked him. Quinn became angry and called them all *corpulent creeps*. That comment enraged a giant pubis fat cell who threw Quinn into a lymph node. A group of white blood cells sensed danger and rushed to save the damaged lymph node. The resulting pandemonium caused several fat cells to be dipped in the Feces Flow Dipping Vat. I dealt with Quinn personally.

Evaluation Results: So we had an aspiring political hack in our group! What next? Quinn was too quick for his own good! I had to deal with him tactfully! Not! Quinn shouldn't have said he wanted to lead his fellow fat cells and then verbally abuse them. A tactic like that only works with some humans! The fat cells are too smart for that!

Final Results: I put Quinn in the Psycho/Sicko Center to de-program his political bullshit! Fat cells have a divine distinction of service to the humans which must continue in a normal manner. Dabbling in politics isn't on Quinn's plate. Quinn was named head orator for the Psycho/Sicko Center. He quips all day long in front of an adoring group of insane fat cells. They call him their: "King of Gibberish!"

Quinn

Dr. R. U. Nuttee: Case # 60
<u>Patient Name</u>: York the Yodeler
Gender: Male   Wt. 0.5 nanogram   Ht. 0.1mm

York was a small fat cell located in his human's tongue. His human developed a devotion to yodeling after a trip to the Swiss alps. It wasn't long before York attempted yodeling. He started to yodel all day long. A big problem occurred when York switched from low pitch singing to high pitch falsetto. He sounded like a braying donkey that had been electrocuted! The screeches York emitted were horrifying! He believed his sounds were magnificent. York requested a *yodel meter* to measure the resonance of his notes. As unbelievable as it sounds such a meter was evidently invented sometime in the 1920s. York's screeching was so unbearable that we ran out of earplugs. I had to put an end to his yodeling from hell. I asked York to come see me for some yodeling tips.

Evaluation Results: Yodeling has a unique history in many cultures. It can be very invigorating when sung properly. York sounded more like a howler than a yodeler. The mournful sounds that came from him set the fat cells on edge. We had enough problems without York's howling which grated on everyone's nerves. This was a tricky situation for me. York may have had an inferiority complex due to his small stature. York probably felt he had gained confidence by his yodeling. For the first time in my career, I lied to a patient. I told York I needed his help to keep peace among the fat cells. I said some fat cells were jealous of York's gift and complained they had no talent. I suggested that he stop yodeling so peace would prevail. York agreed to cease yodeling immediately.

Final Results: Okay, so I was a big fat liar. No fat cell is perfect! To his delight and my dismay, I let York yodel for me once a month. Hey, I'm not always a hard ass!

York

Dr. R. U. Nuttee: Case # 61
<u>Patient Name</u>: Stu & Moe the Stu-Moe Wrestlers
Gender: Males   Wt. 3 nanograms   Ht. 0.2mms

Stu was an extra large ass fat cell who lived in his human's
right buttock cheek. He was the wrestling partner to Moe who
lived in the left buttock cheek. Stu was very proud of his
prowess and paraded about the ass area like a peacock. Even
though Moe was his wrestling partner, Stu zealously guarded
his ass domain and refused to let Moe cross over to the other
cheek. Stu only allowed wrestling exhibitions in the human's
back. In order to enforce the ass boundaries, he made daily
forays to the ass chasm which the fat cells also called the,
scary gigantic crack! Stu wanted to make sure Moe was not
loitering about waiting to sneak over. All was well until the
human developed a badly infected ingrown hair in the area
right above his ass crack. The infection was a festering mass
filled with misbehaving white blood cells who were fighting
among themselves. Stu and Moe both rushed to the area to
evacuate as many fat cells as they could. They barely escaped
with their lives when a needle penetrated the area to inject an
anesthetic for surgery. Stu and Moe looked like pitiful pudge
balls when this calamity ended! I saw them immediately!

Evaluation Results: Stu and Moe were traumatized
by this ordeal. I praised them for their quick thinking and told
them their fellow fat cells would remain safe. I feel a twinge of
guilt for my little fat cell lie. I just couldn't tell Stu and Moe
humans develop medical maladies often without warning. I
wanted them to retain hope for the future. I made arrangements
to see them once a month.

Final Results: Stu and Moe returned to their respective
buttock cheeks. They are heroes to the other fat cells and still
put on wrestling exhibitions in the human's back.

Stu & Moe

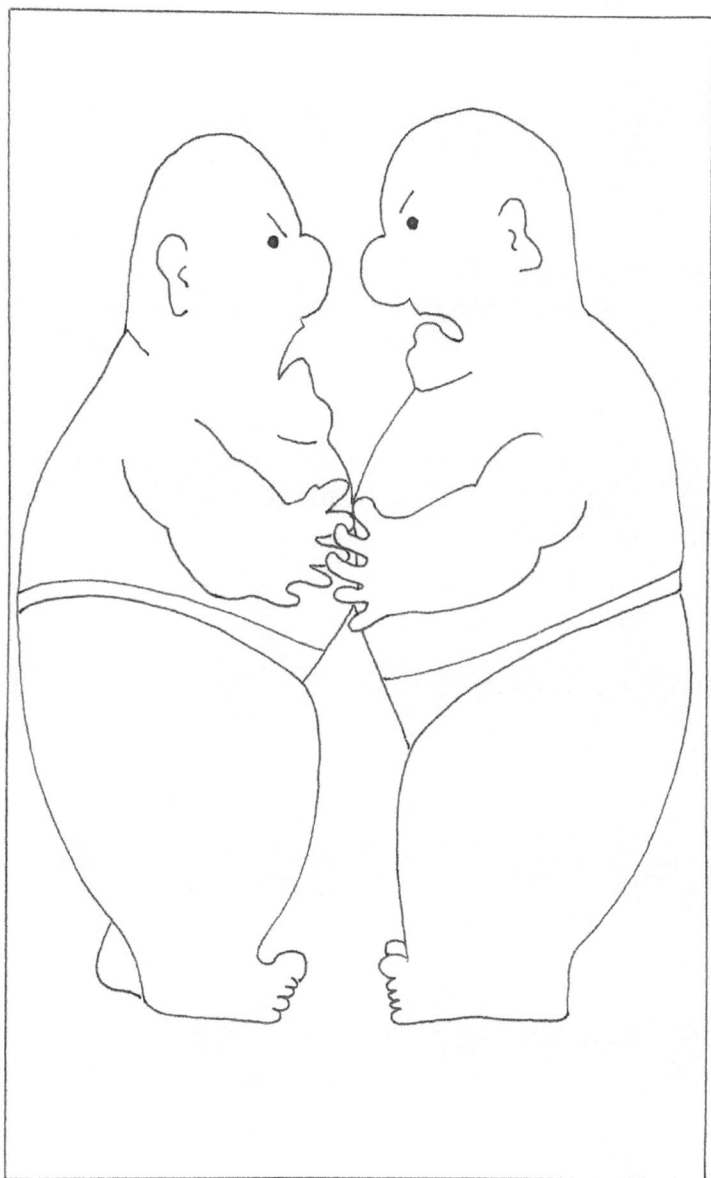

Dr. R. U. Nuttee: Case # 86
<u>Patient Name</u>: Nimbus the Nimble Nincompoop
Gender: Male   Wt. 0.5 nanogram   Ht. 0.1mm

Nimbus was a tiny fat cell who was lodged in the thumb of an author. The human wrote in long hand and spoke the lines as he wrote them. Nimbus heard his human speak of freedom of speech, expression and movement. Those freedoms sounded wonderful to Nimbus and caused him to desire freedom of movement. He did not want to stay in his human's thumb. Nimbus traveled foolishly about his human. Along the way, he spouted off comments designed to irritate his fellow fat cells. A big mistake occurred when Nimbus wedged himself behind one of his human's eyeballs. He triggered a reaction similar to *nystagmus*; which causes the eyeball to twitch back and forth like a spinning top. Fortunately, the eyeball calmed down after a fat cell guard caught Nimbus and carefully removed him from the eye. This nincompoop wasn't so nimble when he was brought to see me!

Evaluation Results: I was just a second away from twirling this little shit like a spinning top! Nimbus might have been the nimblest fat cell on earth but he was also the naughtiest nincompoop. No fat cell is going to cause humans to have spinning eyeballs! When I counseled Nimbus, he flattened himself and attempted to squeeze out through a crack in the wall. I had no choice but to put the son of a bitch in a plastic bag with tiny holes. That nixed his nimbleness nicely!

Final Results: Nimbus showed no remorse for what he had done. That really bugged me! I decided to put his nimbleness to good use. While wearing a tether, Nimbus spends his days cleaning all the fat cell centers and buildings. They haven't been this clean in a long time! In fact, they sparkle like brand new buildings!

Nimbus

Dr. R. U. Nuttee: Case # 89
Patient Name: Orman the Orator
Gender: Male   Wt. 4 nanograms   Ht. 0.3mms

In all my years of counseling fat cells, Orman was the biggest I had ever seen. He lived near the elbow in his human's arm. Orman believed himself to be the greatest orator of all times. He often trailed the other fat cells and spoke passionately about his oratory skills. Many fat cells found Orman's immense size and constant orations too much to bear. Several of them threatened to silence Orman permanently. He became indignant and raced away without paying attention to his direction. Unfortunately, Orman collided with the ulnar nerve and caused a painful spasm in his human's *funny bone*. Orman barely escaped when the human applied an ice pack to the area. Some of the other fat cells there were not as lucky. Several of them were frozen and required intensive care when we thawed them out.

Evaluation Results: I was ready to sew Orman's mouth shut when I heard about this catastrophe. I was also furious with the fat cells who threatened him. Since Orman acted out of fear, I withheld severe punishment. However, he needed to know many fat cells considered him obnoxious. I made it clear that his pride caused a horrendous accident in which several of his fellow fat cells almost perished. Orman hung his head in shame and promised to curtail his orations.

Final Results: I sent Orman to the Psycho/Sicko Center to give this episode a chance to blow over. I didn't want any of the fat cells with freezer burn to come after Orman. I had to be careful or those fat cells might have revolted. After a few days, I put Orman in his human's tongue. The other fat cells there accepted him without question. In fact, they share the gift of gab and spend hours orating with him.

Orman

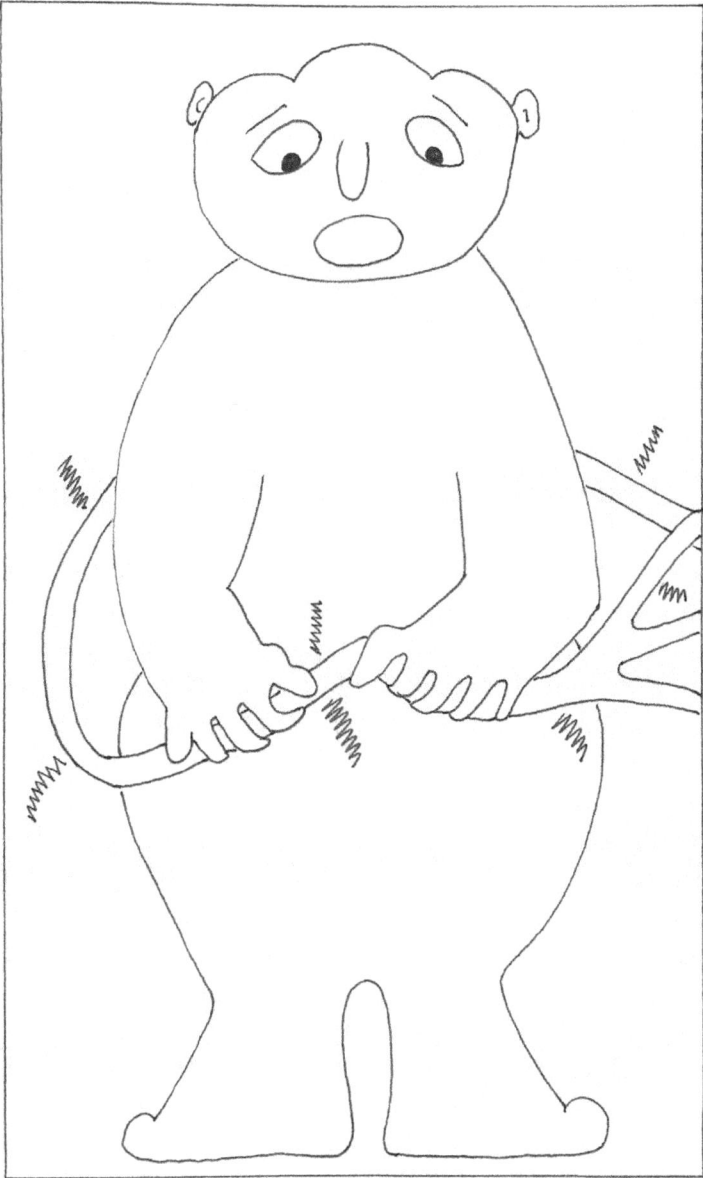

Dr. R. U. Nuttee: Case # 99
<u>Patient Name</u>: Bebe the Belly Bouncer
Gender: Female   Ht. 1 nanogram   Wt. 0.lmm

Bebe was a vivacious abdominal fat cell who bedazzled everyone with her dancing. She had a mischievous habit of bouncing up to her fellow fat cells and bumping them without warning. Most of them loved her antics and many claimed her spontaneity was contagious. Goodwill seemed to follow Bebe wherever she went. Bebe formed a group with some fat cell dancers, and they were called: "Bebe's Belly Bouncers." The dancers entertained all over the abdomen. All was well until a fat cell guard became jealous and accused Bebe of bewitching her fellow fat cells. When no one was looking, the fat cell guard *cellnapped* Bebe and crammed her into a benign belly tumor. Bebe broke free and raced to me for assistance.

Evaluation Results: This horrendous incident almost made me blow my top! The actions of the beastly fat cell guard were alarming and reprehensible. The guard was banished to a *plantar wart* in the human's foot. Fortunately, Bebe was not seriously injured. When she realized I was so furious, Bebe actually tried to make me feel better! I thanked her for being such a good sport. Bebe tried to teach me how to dance. I'm embarrassed to say my two left feet proved I'm not a dancer! I told her the fat cell guards in the belly were going to attend sensitivity seminars. Bebe said their attitudes may improve if they learned how to dance. I asked her to teach them and she agreed. I left it up to Bebe to coordinate the dance lessons.

Final Results: Bebe was a delight! We needed more fat cells like her! She and her "Belly Bouncers" were given *carte blanche* to perform whenever and wherever they want. Bebe taught several fat cell guards how to dance. Sometimes when no one is looking this old doctor pretends he's a dancer too!

Bebe

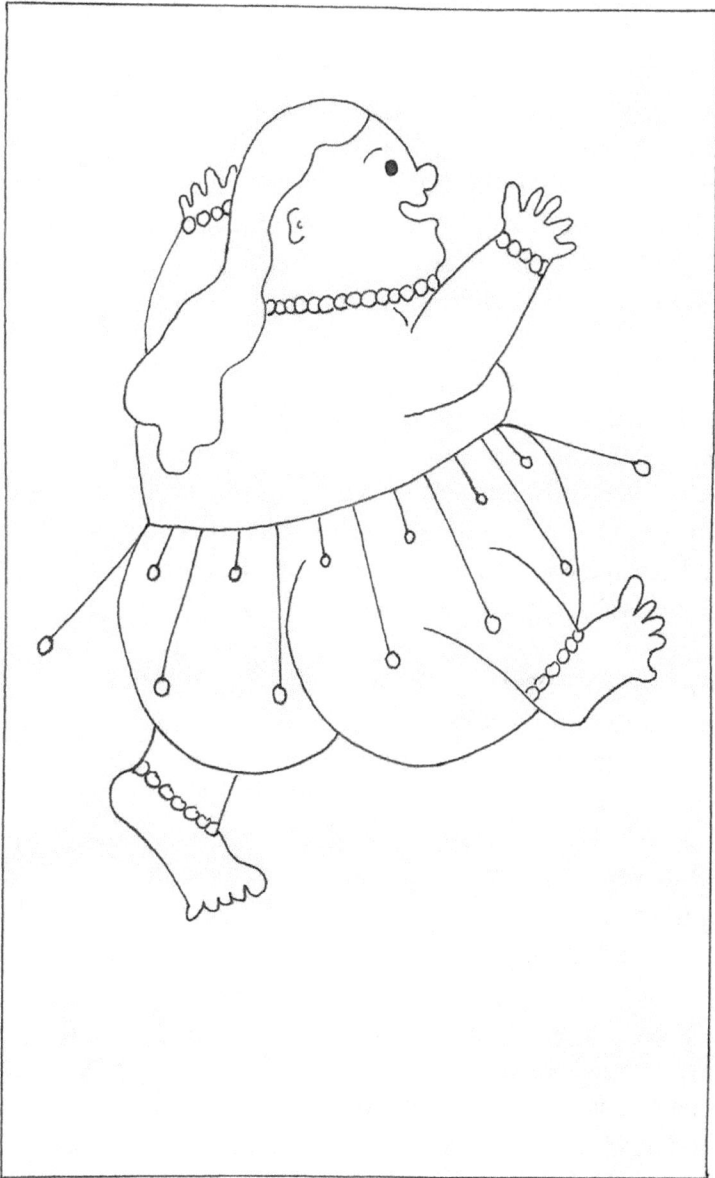

Dr. R. U. Nuttee: Case # 101

Patient Name: Isaiah the Imitator

Gender: Male   Wt. 1 nanogram   Ht. 0.1mm

Isaiah was an underarm fat cell who thought his name literally meant: "I say ah." However, he did not stop with "ah." Isaiah developed a unique garbled language in which he spouted off consecutive words in alphabetical order. His grunts started with ah followed by: "bah, caw, doe, eh, fa, gae, ha, ich, ja, ka, la, me, na, oe, pa, qi, re, sol, ti, ugh, voe, wal, xi, ya and za." If anyone interrupted Isaiah's ramblings, he started over again. Needless to say it was only a matter of time before the other fat cells were ready to strangle Isaiah for his idiotic behavior. Some fat cell guards tried to trick him by reciting Isaiah's words backwards. That was not a good idea! Isaiah screamed insanely! He climbed atop some nearby lymph nodes and tried to pry one loose! One of the well behaved fat cell guards showed compassion to Isaiah. He surrendered to the fat cell guard and willingly came to see me.

Evaluation Results: My frustration with this situation almost caused me to bang my head on the desk. I was one breath away from tattooing on the offending fat cell guards' asses: **Alert Dr. Nuttee First!** Many incidents could have been avoided by handling troubled fat cells properly. After a careful study of Isaiah's mutterings, I detected the musical scales in the words. I sang them and he did too. That was sweet! However, I knew Isaiah needed intensive treatment at the Psycho/Sicko Center.

Final Results: Isaiah was not insane just quirky. He showed remorse for attacking the lymph nodes. After intense therapy his behavior returned to normal. Isaiah requested to stay at the Psycho/Sicko Center so he could read and sing to the other fat cells. They love his made up songs!

Isaiah

Dr. R. U. Nuttee: Case # 217
Patient Name: Emily the Elegant Enchantress
Gender: Female   Wt. 1 nanogram   Ht. 0.1mm

Emily was an elegant ancestral breast fat cell. She possessed a
fairylike quality, and her cell glistened when she told tales to
other fat cells. Emily's voice was exquisite! The fat cells
loved to watch her when she danced and sang songs about the
days of yore. They were enchanted with Emily and called her
their: "Elegant Enchantress!" During one of her performances,
an unruly testosterone laden fat cell disrupted Emily's act. She
grabbed Emily and shook her violently. When some of the
other fat cells tried to save Emily, the vile offender shouted
profane words at them. It took three fat cell guards to pry
Emily loose from the violent attacker. The villainous offender
was doused in the Feces Flow Dipping Vat. The Elegant Emily
was then brought to see me by one of the fat cell guards.

Evaluation Results: No one harms Emily the Elegant
Enchantress! Her attacker was condemned to service in the
rectum. The vile offender now wears the moniker: "Rectum
Recluse!" Emily was badly shaken by her ordeal and yet she
displayed a gracious countenance. Emily was the most
exquisite ancestral breast fat cell I had ever seen. She looked
like a porcelain doll. I could not stop myself from touching her
face to see if she was real. Emily smiled at me. I coughed and
cleared my throat. The two of us spun tales for hours. Emily
showed a resilient nature as we chatted the night away. I felt
confident she would be fine.

Final Results: Emily's mind was filled with exciting tales and
beautiful songs. I asked her to write them down for posterity.
Emily was delighted to do so. She filled three volumes of
books for me. Emily wrote the text and decorated the books
with fanciful art work depicting flora and fauna.

Emily

Dr. R. U. Nuttee: Case # 305
<u>Patient Name</u>: Dimitri the Dimwit
Gender: Male   Wt. 1 nanogram   Ht. 0.1mm

Dimitri started out life as what humans might refer to as a
regular Joe. He was an abdominal cellulite cell who lacked
any outstanding characteristics. All of that changed when his
human started body building. The human became fanatical
about lifting weights and tightening his abdominal area. It
seemed there was a female he was desperate to impress. The
human performed so many sit ups that several fat cells were
displaced. Many of them sought refuge behind the human's rib
cage. No one advised Dimitri to seek a safer locale. One
fateful day, Dimitri was trapped between two tight muscle cells
as the abdomen was relentlessly compressed over and over
again with situps. Dimitri's head was squeezed and his nucleus
was slightly damaged. He was found sitting in front of a mirror
chanting, "me Dimitri, me Dimitri!" I had him brought to me
immediately.

Evaluation Results: The first thing I did was give twenty
kinds of hell to the fat cell guards who should have been on
duty to help Dimitri. It turns out the bastards were too busy
trying to feel up a bosomy male fat cell who somehow
contained extra estrogen. Those creeps who were supposed to
be trustworthy fat cell guards were punished severely. After
several dunks in the Feces Flow Dipping Vat, I relocated them
to the human's rectum. They won't be seeing any bosomy fat
cells down there.

Final Results: Dimitri needed tender loving care! I made sure
he received it along with physical and mental rehabilitation at
the Psycho/Sicko Center. Dimitri improved rapidly. He reads
to the other patients everyday. Dimitri's demeanor has a
calming effect on the other fat cells.

Dimitri

Dr. R. U. Nuttee: Case # 408

<u>Patient Name</u>: Donal the Deluder

Gender: Male   Wt. 2 nanograms   Ht. 0.2mms

Donal was a large fat cell who resided in the palm of his human's hand. Without warning, he became delusional and considered taking over his fellow fat cells. An uncanny coincidence helped Donal make up his mind. His human mentioned Scottish names in a world history lecture. When Donal heard his name meant *world leader*, he decided to follow his destiny. He began deluding other fat cells by claiming to be their leader. Donal successfully tricked many of them into following his orders. He began to shift fat cells to other areas of the body. Donal carelessly took a bunch of fat cells up to the muscular area of the eye and caused *diplopia* (double vision). He was apprehended and dipped repeatedly in the Feces Flow Dipping Vat. After Donal was thoroughly cleaned, he was brought to see me.

Evaluation Results: Donal's punishment didn't slow him down much. As he entered my office, Donal actually commanded me to bow down! It would be a cold day in hell before I bowed down to a dunderhead such as Donal! My refusal to do so caused him to throw a chair at me. Luckily, two fat cell guards were near. Donal was quickly overpowered and strapped into a strait jacket. I let him seethe while I planned his future.

Final Results: Donal tricked and intimidated other fat cells into behaving badly. They were given a warning and put on probation. I was not as lenient with Donal! How could I be? I had to make an example of him. I transferred Donal to the small intestine where he was unmercifully squeezed during *peristalsis* (digestive movement). Donal's days of deluding other fat cells were over!

Donal

Dr. R. U. Nuttee: Case # 410
Patient Name: Aaron the Arrogant Analyst
Gender: Male   Wt. 2 nanograms   Ht. 0.2mms

Aaron was a big arrogant abdominal fat cell. As soon as he arrived in the belly, Aaron began controlling some of his fellow fat cells. He arrogantly claimed to know all about psychoanalysis. Aaron made the fat cells line up. With a look of superiority on his face, he marched up and down the line of fat cells. Aaron said he would analyze, scrutinize and then verbalize their abnormalities. He claimed the fat cells were lucky to have him for their analyst and said they no longer needed Dr. Nuttee. Aaron invented medical conditions and claimed some fat cells were afflicted with them. One fat cell was told he had *nucleus numbing*; another had *lumpy lipids*. The worst diagnosis was *mitochondrial melting*. By the time Aaron was finished with his diatribe, many fat cells were shaking with fear. He felt some fear of his own when four fat cell guards took him to the Feces Flow Dipping Vat per my instructions. After Aaron's arrogance was doused, he was brought to my office immediately.

Evaluation Results: I was outraged and affronted by Aaron! How dare he usurp my position as psychiatrist to the fat cells. Aaron smirked as he slinked into my office. I wanted to slap that smirk off his face. However, I didn't want to lose my cool. Aaron had no medical training of any kind. I forbade him to ever play doctor again. Aaron glared at me and said he would do what ever he wanted. I sent him to the anus for punishment. After two weeks, Aaron begged for release.

Final Results: I relented and gave Aaron a break. He vowed to never break the rules again. Aaron was allowed to work in one of my labs. He did a good job of cleaning and sterilizing my beakers and microscope slides.

Aaron

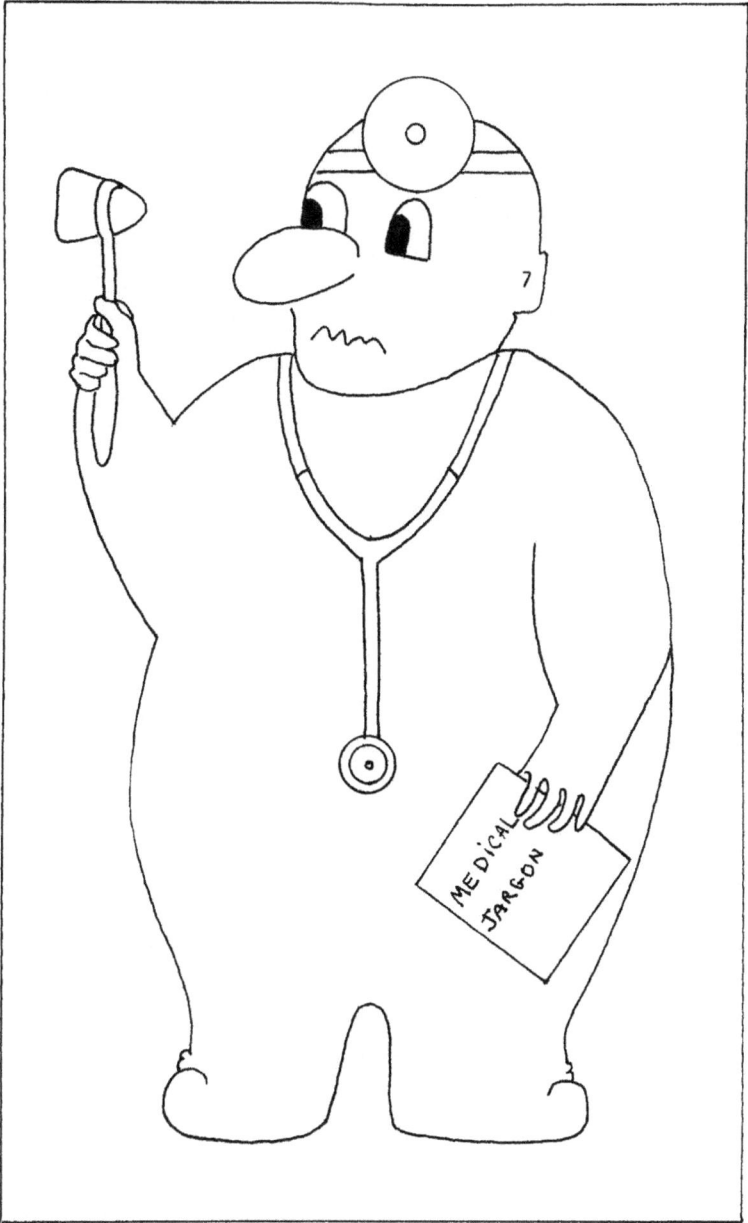

Dr. R. U. Nuttee: Case # 508
<u>Patient Name</u>: Alan the Artist
Gender: Male   Wt. 2 nanograms   Ht. 0.2mms

There is an old saying: "He's was born with a silver spoon in his mouth." In Alan's case it could be: "He was born with a paintbrush in his hand." As soon as he arrived in his human's forearm, Alan began to paint. His artistic style was big and bold like him. I gave Alan permission to extract bits of old skin and dried blood cells from his human. Alan carefully ground the stuff up and added a little recycled lipid oil. The paint worked perfectly for his artwork. He painted visions from his dreams and portraits of his fellow fat cells. They were thrilled! Everyone wanted to have their portraits painted. It wasn't long before the recycled lipid oil ran out. Alan knew it was forbidden to use new lipid oil. He was at a loss because he had to stop painting. Alan became disgruntled and discouraged! One night he stole some new lipid oil from the Lipid Recirculation Chamber. One of his friends told me Alan was being dragged to the Feces Flow Dipping Vat. Thankfully, I arrived in time to stop his punishment.

Evaluation Results: Alan was a unique and gifted artist. I was not going to punish him for being creative. I know artists are different from others. Alan had an inner spark that should not be extinguished. He quoted Fat Gogh: "I think of painting in my sleep and when I awake my thoughts become a painting." I confessed a secret to Alan and divulged my desire to be an artist. He offered to teach me how to paint. I thanked him. I told Alan we could only paint with *recycled oil*!

Final Results: We had to wait two months for more recycled oil. After that, I had a glorious time learning how to paint with Alan. My art wasn't spectacular, but it fit in well with all the *crazies* at the Psycho/Sicko Center.

Alan

Dr. R. U. Nuttee: Case # 515
Patient Name: Morwena the Moralist
Gender: Female   Wt. 2 nanograms   Ht. 0.1mm

Morwena wore her morality like a badge of honor. She expected fat cells who were serving a rotation in the index finger with her to do the same. Morwena moralized daily about manners, decorum and etiquette. She followed other fat cells around and took notes about their behavior. The more Morwena pushed her ways, the more she was shunned by other fat cells. Some of them began to call her *Morwhinea* or *Moronwena*. Morwena's situation became grave when she chided some white blood cells who were attempting to contain a nasty infection. Two of them turned on Morwena and smeared her with bacteria from the infection. She was aghast! Morwena lost her decorum and screamed, "you are heinous bastards!" Morwena was so upset, it took her an hour to get to my office.

Evaluation Results: Morwena was covered with bacterial slime when she arrived. Yuck! It took my nurse an hour to de-germify her. I know Morwena had good intentions. After all, our great philosopher Fatocrates said: "Fat cells should live their lives in civilized ways!" Those words serve society well! It wouldn't hurt for all the fat cells to follow them. However, they didn't deserve to be harassed by Morwena. I explained to her the other fat cells were capable of making their own decisions regarding their behavior. Morwena promised to tone down her obsession with manners.

Final Results: Morwena was not insane just over zealous. After attending lessons in self control, she was given a position at the Fatistotle Cellulite Cell Charm Center. Morwena teaches manners and etiquette. Those who meet her say, Morwena is the nicest teacher of them all.

Morwena

Dr. R. U. Nuttee: Case # 520
Patient Name: Lunette the Lunatic
Gender: Female   Wt. 1 nanogram   Ht. 0.1mm

Lunette began her life as a sweet fat cell who was located near the tonsils in her human's throat. Unfortunately, during her human's tonsillectomy, Lunette's nucleus was damaged. Soon after that, she began to exhibit signs of lunacy. Lunette chased other fat cells proclaiming they needed oral surgery. Her speech became inarticulate and barely audible. As Lunette became less coherent, she developed *logorrhea* (an excessive flow of words). During all of this, no one bothered to tell me about Lunette's predicament. When she was discovered pounding upon a fellow fat cell, I was informed of her loony behavior. Lunette refused to see me. As a result, two fat cell guards strapped her to a gurney and brought Lunette to my office.

Evaluation Results: I had a hard time controlling my anger when I saw Lunette on the gurney. Those damn fat cell guards should have informed me sooner about her problem. Lunette had a look of bewilderment on her lovely moon shaped face. She smiled shyly when I told her the name Lunette means *little moon* in French. As a medical doctor, I realize our locations within humans make us vulnerable to medical tragedies. However, that does not make them any easier to accept. I had no choice but to put Lunette in the Psycho/Sicko Center.

Final Results: In honor of her name and with the hopes of making Lunette more comfortable, the nurses and I painted a moon and stars on the ceiling of her room. Lunette's logorrhea was put to good use when she befriended a fellow fat cell who banged drums all day long. The cadence of Lunette's flowing speech, coupled with the drums, made a unique sort of music.

170

Lunette

171

Dr. R. U. Nuttee: Case # 601
Patient Name: Zelda the Zany
Gender: Female   Wt. 1.5 nanograms   Ht. 0.1mm

Zelda was a facial fat cell who had more zeal and zaniness than any other fat cell I've ever known. She loved to play practical jokes on other fat cells. They all loved her zany attitude. As Zelda's popularity increased so did her following. It was very nice to witness the goodwill shared by the fat cells. However, the pleasant situation turned to mayhem when fat cells from other areas descended on Zelda's location and demanded to meet her. The huge influx of thousands of fat cells caused a gigantic lump to rise on the human's facial cheek. Nothing like this had ever happened before! I rushed to the spot and admonished the offenders with a warning to never leave their posts again. It took two hours for the fat cell guards to return the trouble makers to their proper locations. Zelda was instructed to meet with me.

Evaluation Results: What a circus! What a horrible carnival! I felt like the only thing missing was the elephant poop! See what happened when notoriety took hold of a fat cell. Zelda was wonderful, but a fat cell cannot be allowed to wreak havoc! I still shudder to think of all the thousands of fat cells we could have lost due to that monstrous mess. I know fat cells want to have fun, but it is imperative for them to maintain their positions! The rules are necessary to protect the humans. If the rules seem too strict for the fat cells. . . too bad!

Final Results: Zelda was not totally to blame. The fat cell guards should have done a better job. Zelda apologized for the chaos and promised to tone down her zaniness. Thankfully, no one was hurt! I was lenient with Zelda. She organized a group of students and teaches them theater arts at the Fatistotle Cellulite Cell Curriculum Center.

Zelda

Dr. R. U. Nuttee: Case # 723

<u>Patient Name</u>: John the Jolly Juggler
Gender: Male   Wt. 1 nanogram   Ht. 0.1mm

John was a jolly fat cell who was located in the palm of his human's hand. He was full of energy. John was an amazing athlete with fast hands. We found out how quickly John could move when an unusual accident happened to some other fat cells. It occurred when some renegade white blood cells tore through a group of fat cells. Three fat cells slipped and their lipid readers were flung up into the air. John miraculously caught all of the lipid readers and began to joyously juggle them. Another fat cell rushed up and called John, a *jolly juggler*! The name stuck and John became an expert juggler. However, it wasn't long before he became bored with juggling the same objects over and over. John went in search of new items to juggle. A fat cell guard caught him in an ear canal. John was forming ear wax into balls to use for juggling. I spoke with him the following day.

Evaluation Results: I purposely placed three balls on my desk before John's arrival. I wanted to see what he would do. John showed restraint when he entered my office; however, he could not hide the nervous twitch which caused his hand to jump about. John wanted those balls! A giant smile lit his face when I tossed them to him and said, "juggle John!" His skill was extraordinary. John was a delight to watch. I could see why he wanted new items to toss about. It was ingenious of him to think of shaping balls from ear wax. Not only was he athletic, but John was smart too! With his help, I tried juggling. I fumbled about and broke a window! No more juggling for this doctor!

Final Results: John is a guest teacher at the Psycho/Sicko Center. His students love to learn juggling from him!

John

Dr. R. U. Nuttee: Case # 808
<u>Patient Name</u>: Urania the Ufologist
Gender: Female   Wt. 1 nanogram   Ht. 0.1mm

Urania was a fat cell who was located in the protective fat pad in her human's brow bone. Thanks to that location she was able to see many things. Urania eventually became spellbound by her human's interest in UFOs. Since the name Urania means *heavenly* in the Greek language, she probably believed it was her destiny to study all things celestial. It wasn't long before Urania dubbed herself a *Ufologist*! Unfortunately, Urania's anticipation for sights unseen took her over the edge. She insanely claimed UFOs were flying around the fat cells! Urania said a shiny blue light had enshrouded her. Some fat cells became fed up and called her, *Urania the Insania* and *Urania with Ufomania*. She asked to see me after a fat cell threw a tiny artificial UFO at her.

Evaluation Results: This may have seemed like a comical situation. Not in my eyes! And not on my shift! What if this became a craze and all fat cells wanted to throw around tiny UFOs? If I have said it once, I have said it a thousand times: "NOTHING CAN INTERFERE WITH THE HUMANS' *HOMEOSTASIS*!" The guilty fat cell who threw the tiny UFO had an out of this world experience in the Feces Flow Dipping Vat! Urania believed UFOs were after her. I told her the only UFOs we had were Unidentified Fat Objects in the Psycho/Sicko Center. As a ruse to get Urania there, I asked her to help me with the other fat cells. After I guaranteed her safety, Urania agreed.

Final Results: Urania was officially dubbed the Ufologist of the Psycho/Sicko Center. She spends her days identifying and cataloging her fellow fat cell patients and any UFOs that happen to come flying by.

Urania

Dr. R. U. Nuttee: Case # 920
Patient Name: Raziela the Radiant Rebel
Gender: Female   Wt. 1 nanogram   Ht. 0.1mm

Raziela was a radiant fat cell who was located inside her human's upper lip. Rebellion was on Raziela's mind from the moment she came out of the fat cell depot. She glowed with an unusual radiance which caused other fat cells to flock around her. Raziela used her magnetism to cast a spell on them. She convinced them to join her in a rebellion against the fat cell guards. Raziela said rebelling was the only way to achieve the freedom they desired. The revolt caused a physical skirmish which damaged several fat cells. After their capture, Raziela and her cohorts had a dipping party in the Feces Flow Dipping Vat. Raziela was thoroughly cleaned and brought to see me.

Evaluation Results: As soon as Raziela saw me she spat in my face. Lucky for her, she missed me! I was furious! Who the hell did this female demon think she was? I'm sure I had a maniacal look in my eyes when I calmly said, "What's the matter? Didn't you enjoy your dipping party? Next time we'll try to have balloons for you!" Raziela screamed and lunged at me. She coughed and sputtered when some fat cell guards held her down. Raziela burst into tears. My conscience chided me for my unprofessional behavior. A doctor should not bait his patients. I regretted the comments I made and apologized to her. She nodded in acceptance. I took several hours to explain to Raziela that fat cells could change their locations but never change their stations in life. I told her fat cells must follow the course God ordained for them.

Final Results: Raziela was taken to the Psycho/Sicko Center. I counseled her for months and her attitude improved. Raziela's radiance returned and she volunteered to help other fat cells achieve positive goals. It was nice to see her happy!

Raziela

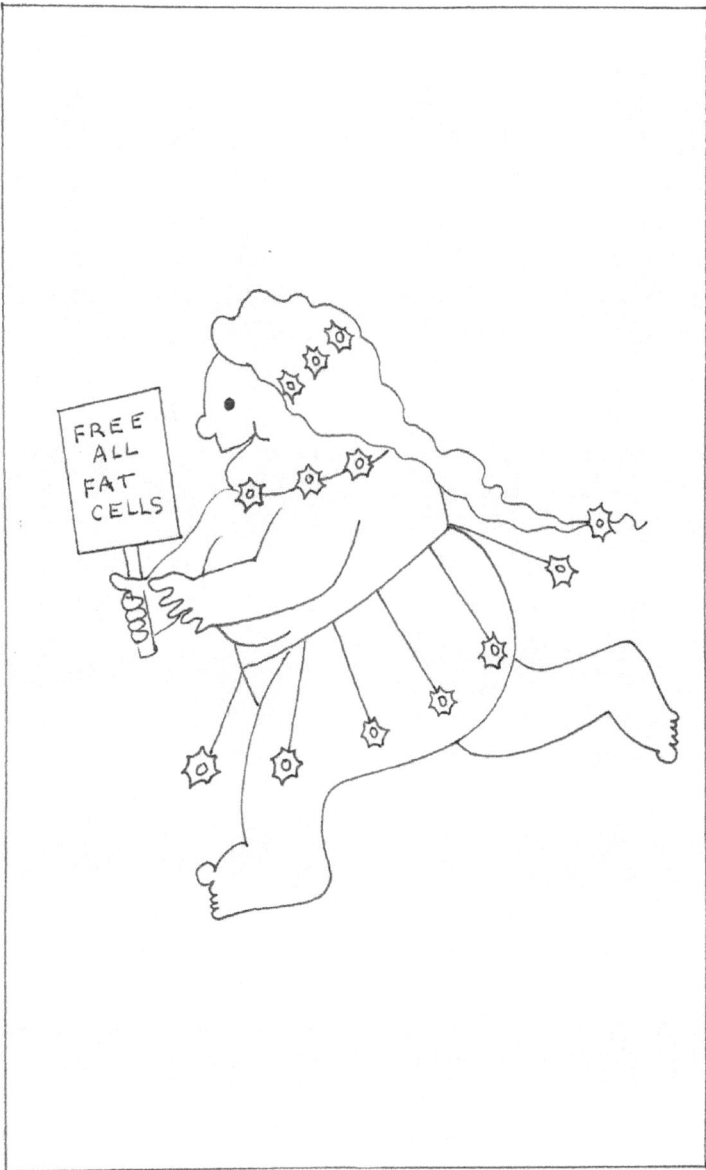

Dr. R. U. Nuttee: Case # 930

<u>Patient Name</u>: Elric the Eccentric Echoer

Gender: Male   Wt. 1 nanogram   Ht. 0.1mm

Elric was an oddball who lived in his human's upper rib cage.
This location coupled with his huge ears, allowed Elric to hear
all sorts of sounds. He became obsessed with reverberations
from the heart and lungs. Elric claimed they sounded like
echoes. He decided to add tones of his own to the mix. Elric
attempted to send echoes across his area. With each try, he
called, "hello, am I audible?" None of the other fat cells
bothered to answer Elric. He called hello over and over again.
Since no one responded, Elric decided he was in an echoless
area. He moved and stood on the *sternum* which sits in the
middle of the rib cage. Elric shouted, "hello, hello! Am I
audible, do I have audibility?" When this didn't work, Elric
jumped from rib to rib shouting, "am I audible?" Two fat cell
guards confirmed his audibility when Elric was taken to the
Feces Flow Dipping Vat. His screeches of horror echoed
throughout the area! I spoke with him later.

Evaluation Results: Elric was still erratically emitting echoes
when he came through my door. I shook my head and thought,
what fresh hell is this? I dramatically took out some ear plugs
and put them in my ears. A perplexed look crossed Elric's face.
The look in his eyes was beyond sadness. Damn, double damn,
I felt like a heel. Elric didn't realize what he did was wrong,
and he didn't have willful intent to do wrong. I was guilty of
prejudging him and I knew better! I removed the ear plugs and
asked Elric to call out echoes. I complimented him on his rich
baritone voice. We came up with a scheme.

Final Results: As a favor to me, Elric sings and calls echoes to
fat cells in the Psycho/Sicko Center. They all think he is the
greatest. Some of them even learned how to echo!

Elric

Dr. R. U. Nuttee: Case # 938
Patient Name: Wayne the Whacky Whacko
Gender: Male   Wt. 1 nanogram   Ht. 0.1mm

Sometimes in the scheme of things, a fat cell occasionally comes out of a cell depot with a physical abnormality. Such was the case with Wayne the Whacko. His large head looked as though it had been whacked by a heavy object. As a result of his deformity, Wayne was labeled a whacko. He wanted friends but the other fat cells avoided him. One day on a whim Wayne tried to be witty. His jokes were ignored. Wayne wondered why no one laughed at his wisecracks. He decided to act whackier. While whistling, Wayne paraded among the fat cells. He gently whacked each fat cell and told them to laugh. After his tenth try, a fat cell laughed. Wayne had won over a friend. He taught his new companion how to whistle. They began to demonstrate whistling techniques to other fat cells. Whistling became popular! Wayne's status changed. His fat cell fans renamed him Wayne the Whistling Wizard.

Evaluation Results: Wayne was not insane just misunderstood. Other fat cells harshly judged Wayne and yet he still persevered. Once fat cells saw how talented Wayne was, they acted friendly to him. I was relieved when Wayne was treated fairly by his peers. I met with him because I wanted to learn how to whistle. He taught me well!

Final Results: Wayne was a good sport! He agreed to teach whistling to the patients in the Psycho/Sicko Center. It wasn't long before hundreds of fat cells puckered up and whistled. As a result some spittle flew around. The nurses were not amused. I told them whistling made the lunatics happy and more cooperative. The nurses and I devised a plan for the fat cells to whistle while they cleaned the tile floors. The nurses were thrilled! They learned how to whistle too!

Wayne

Dr. R. U. Nuttee: Case # 1001
<u>Patient Name</u>: Spica the Spirited Scamp
Gender: Female   Wt. 1 nanogram   Ht. 0.lmm

Spica was the embodiment of a scamp. She scampered about her human's back like an elusive spirit. Spica's location along the spine enabled her to hear the flow of the spinal fluid. She decided it would be fun to follow its path. As Spica skipped up and down the spine, she scrutinized her path for anything that might be amiss. When other fat cells complained about her freedom of movement, Spica claimed she was safeguarding the area. Some other fat cells followed her. Within a matter of minutes, three fat cell guards put an end to everyone's travels. Spica sulked! She couldn't contain herself! Spica silently slipped away for one more shenanigan. She sped along the spine as if there were demons after her. Spica ran head first into some monstrous muscle cells. She screamed as they attempted to assimilate her into their bodies. Spica was rescued by a group of fat cell guards who were on patrol in the area. She was in rough shape when I saw her.

Evaluation Results: Spica's condition was worse than anyone realized. She wasn't insane before the attack but the muscle mishandling may have sent her over the edge. Spica's nucleus was badly damaged by those moronic muscle cells. They endured some rough handling of their own at the Feces Flow Dipping Vat. I treated Spica gently and promised her the best of care. She was placed in the Psycho/Sicko Center.

Final Results: Spica's case shook me to the core! I forced myself to focus on her recovery because I really wanted to mangle those muscle cells. I kept a positive attitude so Spica would feel hope and encouragement. She made a steady recovery. When I saw Spica teaching other fat cells how to scamper and skip, I knew she was going to be alright!

Spica

Dr. R. U. Nuttee: Case # 1020

Patient Name: Luke the Lively Lyricist
Gender: Male   Wt. 1 nanogram   Ht. 0.1mm

While in the fat cell depots, most fat cells wait patiently until they are called for service. Not Luke! He squirmed incessantly! We found out why. Luke was bursting with song! His voice was magical. When he penned lyrics about his fellow fat cells, they called Luke a musical genius! Nothing escaped his keen mind. Luke had the ability to artfully assess his fellow fat cells. He knew how to make them feel better about themselves through his songs. It was unusual for me to do so, but I felt compelled to record some of Luke's lyrics from his songs for his file. Here are some samples of his work:

****

When I think of thee,
it sets my heart free.
I know I shall always be,
happy when you are near me.

****

Stand by and I shall sing you a song,
your duties can wait this won't take long.
Our friendship forever will make us strong,
as we go forward together against the throng.

****

Merrily, merrily I say to thee
come along and dance with me.
We will twirl and twirl for all to see,
as we spin across the floor gracefully.

****

Laughter helps to heal the heart,
it lifts the spirit so you can start
to feel better and make sorrow depart.

****

Every bit of happiness you bring to me,
helps me to see quite clearly,
love is the gift that sets my spirit free.

****

The wondrous thoughts I have of you,
and our love that is so true,
makes me feel young and new.

****

Whether in the sunshine bright,
or the darkness of the night,
I feel tender delight,
to know you're my guiding light.

****

There is so much beauty in this place,
I love being a part of the human race.
My memories here no one can erase,
since I live within a human filled with grace.

Evaluation Results: Luke was a breath of fresh air for this old doctor. He is not insane. I have included Luke in this compendium to show others that certain fat cells can make a big difference in our lives. I keep Luke's file handy because reading his lyrics fill me with hope! I feel the gray areas of despair lift away from me every time I read his file. I feel even better when I hear Luke sing. I have seen so much tragedy in my life that it makes me eager to appreciate the talents of others. Of all our fat cell singers, Luke is my favorite!

Final Results: It is not often that I reveal my feelings in a patient's medical file. Of course, I have expressed my reactions to various patients. With Luke, I feel as though I have exposed my soul. I just cannot help myself. The verses of his songs deliver hope and understanding; which are the two qualities fat cells need. Luke holds monthly sing-alongs for the resident fat cells at the Psycho/Sicko Center.

Luke

Dr. R. U. Nuttee: Case # 1201

Patient Name: Posy the Poetess
Gender: Female   Wt. 1.5 nanograms   Ht. 0.1mm

Posy was a beautiful ancestral breast fat cell who had the marvelous ability to poetize anything. Her poems were often insightful. She encouraged her fellow fat cells to reflect on all aspects of life. Posy came to see me after a period of introspection caused her to have great sadness. I have included some of her poems for this file. My evaluation and final results follow Posy's poetry.

"Twist of Fate"

What cruel twist of fate brought me to this place,
where I exist as a nameless face?
I'm only trying to help the human race,
when it's my very presence they wish to erase.

"Human Dwelling"

I am but a fat cell hidden within this human hell,
my presence isn't tolerated very well.
I know upon sadness I shouldn't dwell,
but I have doubts I cannot quell,
because I'm only a fat cell.

"Donuts"

I know I caused you extra weight,
it seems to be both our fate,
thanks to all those extra donuts you just ate!

"The Method"

The method is thine,
so when thee dine,
extra helpings thee should decline,
so your weight stays in line.

"Lonely Fat Cells"

Dear humans we must proclaim,
you have a life and a name.
We shall always be the same,
lonely fat cells filled with shame,
since we receive all of your blame.

"Give up the Fight"

You may as well give up the fight,
because you possess a healthy appetite,
don't fret and worry over a tasty bite,
it's okay if your willpower takes flight.

"Food Indulgences"

I will not be treated with such disdain,
so I request that you refrain,
for blaming me when it's weight you gain,
you are the one who has to abstain,
from food indulgences which cause you to complain.

"Calories"

Calories, calories they are everywhere,
I wish I could get them out of my hair.
It really is so unfair,
to know they are waiting there,
to stand up and proudly declare,
"watch out don't eat more than your share!"

"Freedom Song"

We are a billion strong.
We are where we belong.
Help us and come along,
while we sing our freedom song:

"Fat cells are totally true,
fat cells are good for you.
please don't question what we do,
we support you through and through."

"Plumplicious"

She was a plumplicious fat cell,
who put her human under a spell,
things were going very well,
until another human said, "Oh do tell!"
"You've grown as big as the Liberty Bell,"
causing the plump human to enter diet hell.

"Insensitivity"

Attention… some humans display animosity,
when they shed their civility,
and behave without propriety,
as they exhibit audacity,
and blatant insensitivity,
crowned with an air of superiority,
while escorted with negativity,
they make it their priority,
to question the viability,
of a plump person's credibility,
as if said plump person has no compatibility,
due to their obesity,
which causes unacceptability,
due to the uncivil groups vanity,
which encourages an affinity,
to grasp conformity,
as they march ahead with conventionality,
so they may proclaim exclusivity,
for their members who hold no generosity,
as they withhold equality,
never mind the lack of magnanimity,
they behave with pomposity,
and a lack of originality,
as they claim with false validity:
"To befriend a plump person would be a calamity!"

Evaluation Results: Oh boy, Posy's case was one that sent shivers down my spine! Posy obviously was not insane. I did some inner soul searching because I was afraid I may not be able to help her. Of course, I knew that was very narcisstic of me. However, sometimes a little self-doubt spurs one to try harder to find answers. The answers were there alright. . . in vivid black and white. Posy was an anomaly. Her sensitivity made her aware of things that escaped the other fat cells. I have never said this about another fat cell (besides myself of course), Posy would make a superior human being. I wanted so badly to tell her my feelings but to do so would have saddened her to a point of total desperation. Posy's poems were an excellent outlet for her frustration with life. Posy felt as though she was to blame for her human's weight issues. I decided to be blunt about some aspects of the human condition.

Final Results: Posy was very sad and depressed the first time I counseled her. I used a little humor to brighten her mood and I think it helped. I told Posy humans had all sorts of eccentricities which tied into their eating patterns. I said the humans were responsible for what they ate. I let Posy know that as humans developed a dependency upon machinery, they became less active. She was interested in my chart depicting human anatomy. I showed Posy the ways the human body was perfectly designed for athletic movement. We discussed the details of fat cells, muscles, ligaments and tendons along with the bones that enable humans to move efficiently. I told her I believed humans should be more active. Posy said she would spend her days dancing if she were a human. We laughed! We decided that even if the humans didn't want to exercise, we would! I appointed Posy a leader of physical activities at the Fatistotle Cellulite Cell Curriculum Center. She spends her days happily dancing and exercising with her fellow fat cells.

Posy

Introduction to
Fat Cell Musings

Over the years fat cells have dutifully provided support, energy and protection for humans. It was only natural for fat cells to be absorbed into all facets of the humans' lives. Their positions in humans enabled them to be keen observers of human behavior. Due to their close relationships with their hosts, some fat cells emulated their humans. The close contact, coupled with their astute observations turned many fat cells into quasi-philosophers. They volunteered to pen their thoughts in a section called: "Musings of the Fat Cells!"
Their musings follow.

Musings of a Fat Cell
in a *Foodie*

1. Yippee, she's a connoisseur of chocolate!

2. I feel like I have died and gone to fat cell heaven!

3. There is always something delicious on her plate!

4. I love what she reads: "Cookbooks!"

5. I never thought I would say this about a human: "She's perfect!"

6. She knows life is short so she makes the most of every bite!

7. She's too good to be true, she makes cookies every week!

8. She knows the cooking axiom: "Fat carries the flavor" and she uses it!

9. The word *diet* is taboo in her house.

10. She is *plumplicious*!

Musings of a Fat Cell
in a Nutritionist

1. She might call it good nutrition, but sometimes it seems like starvation!

2. I think her nose would be less out of joint if she ate some chocolate once in a while!

3. She is wrong. . . doughnuts are good food!

4. Please just this once, put some butter and sour cream on that baked potato!

5. Her taste buds are all programmed for non-fat food!

6. She needs to have her cake and eat it too!

7. Her stomach has shrunk down to the size of a kidney bean!

8. She never fantasizes about food and that cannot be normal!

9. I would give anything to be in a plump person!

10. She threw out a box of Valentine's candy! If that is not insane, then what is?

Musings of a Fat Cell
in a Psychiatrist

1. Sometimes I think he is a fruitcake, other times I am sure of it!

2. Regardless of what he thinks, it is not about sex, it is about food!

3. He keeps his emotions in check. That's why he's about to burst!

4. He keeps his patients waiting so long, they have time to develop a new affliction. Hey, something has got to keep the money rolling in!

5. He eats the same thing for breakfast everyday. It is so borrrrrring!

6. It's impossible to be politically correct in the world of psychiatry. If he did, he would just go in circles. Oh wait, he does that anyway!

7. I hate oatmeal! Would it kill him to have a pancake with syrup once in awhile?

8. He's wound up tighter than a spring. When he snaps it is going to be. . . *boing, boing, boing* city around here!

9. He's so wrapped up in his medical journals, he has not eaten in three days. . . and he calls his patients crazy!

10. This rotation is cruel and unusual punishment! I want a transfer! Now!

Musings of a Fat Cell
in a Cowboy

1. Lord help me, he eats nothing but beans and jerky! Yuck!

2. You have never known stench, until you have smelled his boots!

3. Couldn't he say you instead of y'all just once?

4. I thought I could never hate the sound of a harmonica. Thanks to him, I do now!

5. He does not know what a *gourmet* is! Why am I not surprised?

6. There is no such thing as a five-star chuck wagon!

7. There is just no way to get this horse smell off of him!

8. I hereby ban the words chow, mess and grub from my vocabulary.

9. The full moon looks like a pie! Too bad the ones out here are only cow-pies!

10. God, please put me in a *Foodie* next time!

Musings of a Fat Cell
in a Female Movie Star

1. I think the line originally read: "Why don't you come up and feed me sometime?"

2. If she's a natural blonde, I'm a muscle cell!

3. Okay, the Oscars are over now. Quit the diet and eat!

4. If she has one more face lift, her mouth will be up on her forehead!

5. Put that size 2 back on the rack, you're at least a size 10!

6. She doesn't have one vain bone in her body! She has 206 of them!

7. Forget diamonds, food is a girl's best friend!

8. From one fat cell to another, those are not her real boobs!

9. There isn't a diet on earth that she hasn't tried!

10. I'm beginning to think actresses are a new breed of crazy!

Musings of a Fat Cell
in a Geriatric Male

1. Positively no more erectile dysfunction pills!

2. Skipping a bath three days in a row is not acceptable!

3. Vodka is not a food, moron!

4. Cooked cabbage is not intended for senior citizens.

5. Get out of the golf cart and walk!

6. Sex ain't going to happen so get over it!

7. You have to change your underpants more then once a week!

8. Holey socks do not mean you have religion!

9. Watch those feet of yours, your toenails shouldn't have to be trimmed with a chain saw! Duh!

10. Put something on under that trench coat or you're not going out!

Musings of a Fat Cell
in a Ballerina

1. If she gets any skinnier, we're all sunk!

2. She weighs herself ten times a day. What does she think, she's gained weight from the air?

3. She's all muscle and I'm paranoid!

4. If I hear the word *plié* one more time, I'm going to kill myself!

5. I hope she comes back as a plump human!

6. Where's a lipid droplet when you need one?

7. I'd like to put some fat in that *arabesque* of hers!

8. She can't be a real human, she's never tasted pizza once!

9. I just want to stuff her full of candy!

10. Thanks to her, I've become so thin I don't recognize myself!

Musings of a Fat Cell
in a Fire-Eater

1. Ouch! Ouch! Ouch!

2. His parents must be so proud! Not!

3. This takes insanity to a whole new level!

4. He never met a flame he didn't like!

5. His breath always smells like burnt rubber!

6. His gal says he's a red hot lover!

7. One wrong move and he'll have toasted tonsils!

8. See what happens when you play with fire!

9. His favorite saying is: "Fire in the hole!"

10. What's that smell. . . Help! I'm on fire!

Musings of a Fat Cell
in a Compulsive Dieter

1. What did I do to deserve this?

2. Don't walk past those cookies, eat them, eat them!

3. Radishes suck! There's no two ways about it!

4. So this is what the dawn of time was like!

5. I abhor the phrase, *count calories*!

6. Surely, one potato chip would not hurt her!

7. Boy, humans sure do become crabby when
   they are on a diet!

8. She has *ODD*, *O*bsessive *D*ieter's *D*isorder!

9. Her psychiatrist told her there is nothing wrong with
   her. What a quack!

10. If I had a nickel for every time she refused a dessert,
    I would be a millionaire!

Musings of a Fat Cell
in a Skeptic

1. She thinks no one believes a word she says.

2. People say she is friendly but what do they know?

3. She did not get a yearbook. She figured no one was going to sign it anyway!

4. After the psychiatrist heard her problems, he said he could not be bothered with them!

5. She wanted to buy a new dress but she felt she lacked good taste!

6. She felt she was wishy-washy but then again she wasn't sure!

7. She wanted to be a poet but her words stopped her!

8. She finds it easier to have discussions that lead nowhere!

9. She is from a long line of doubting Thomas's!

10. She would like to have a plan but she's sure it would fail!

Musings of a Fat Cell
in a Big Toe

1. No, no do not put on those stinky socks you wore yesterday!

2. Trim my toe nail already, it's growing into me!

3. Enough with the narrow pointed boots, I'm crammed up against four other guys in here!

4. Buy your own pair of bowling shoes. I'm tired of smelling someone else's stinky feet!

5. Oh no, I think I feel the itch of athlete's foot!

6. Stop going barefoot! I don't want to get stung by a bee again!

7. Why does it feel like I am bearing the brunt of all of his weight when he goes bowling?

8. Every time he has too much to drink, he stubs me! I have run out of names to call him!

9. The last time he kicked a football, it hurt like hell! He needs to find a different sport!

10. I am a very important digit! Don't forget it!

Musings of a Fat Cell
in a Stripper

1. Boy, it's crowded in these big boobs!

2. Her thighs are too muscular! Where are our cellulite cell cousins?

3. I'm getting sick and tired of that pole! It's cold when she rubs up against that thing!

4. Oh no, this guys got arms like an octopus! They're everywhere at once!

5. Damn her and her diet! She cancelled the pizza again!

6. Hey it's drafty down here in this G-string!

7. Look out, here comes the guy with the big paws!

8. And to think she took ballet to do this!

9. If she gets any thinner, they'll think she's the pole!

10. Oh come on, take a bite of that chocolate cake! You just worked out for three hours! You know you want it!

Introduction to
Snippets & *Quipetes*

    During their years of service to the humans, fat cells were exposed to a variety of words. Most human words became the vernacular of fat cells too. As fat cells picked up words and phrases from humans they even coined some new words and slogans of their own.

    Fat cells are proud to present some of their ideas, thoughts, requests, likes and dislikes.

Snippets & *Quipetes*

1. Humans spend time trying to do some things, which turn into other things, soon other things eclipse some things so that eventually humans forget the original things they wanted to do!

2. Pucker up and whistle!

3. I'm more than a fat cell in a toe. I'm an *Ambulating Aid*!

4. When humans make a mistake, they pick themselves up and keep on trying!

5. *S.O.S.* . . . send all sauerkraut to the moon!

6. A giggle a day should be mandatory!

7. Please, no more black beans! The methane is killing us!

8. If the sound of a human's laughter was art, it's paintings would be the best in the world!

9. Fat is *fatabulous*!

10. I just want to be kissed once!

11. Leave the jalapeño peppers alone! This ass is on fire!

12. When humans laugh, good will grows!

13. Let your taste buds do their jobs and enjoy your food!

14. Personally, I'm glad humans have two funny bones!

15. We love farmers because they grow food!

16. When humans make one another laugh, it makes us proud!

17. The kitchen is our favorite place to be!

18. Sing a song it helps the spirit stay strong!

19. Television is acceptable when a cooking program is on!

20. Wow, it's wonderful that holidays incorporate fancy foods!

21. I know we help to make humans laugh, but they really are a bunch of comical geniuses too!

22. When humans are well fed, they are more creative!

23. Sharing good food could probably solve some arguments!

24. I love the word whimsical. I'm glad humans create all sorts of items like balloons, kites, toys, and other stuff that brings fun into their lives!

25. If a human breaks their funny bone, does it mean they can't laugh anymore?

26. Who is the fat lady? When is she going to sing?

27. Chips without dip are kind of plain!

28. Pickles are funny looking little green things!

29. Who would have guessed a confection like cotton candy could be made. Thank you humans!

30. Fat cells never brood, we're too busy thinking of food!

31. If humans would walk as much as they talk, they might feel better!

32. Personally, I think a female with curves is sexy!

33. If you can write a joke, you're one lucky bloke!

34. When a granola bar doesn't hit the spot, chocolate comes in handy!

35. If you have never danced, there's no time like the present!

36. When you check yourself out in the mirror, be sure to give yourself a smile!

37. Put you nose to good use and stop and smell some fresh baked bread once in a while!

38. If you don't have someone to kiss, suck on a piece of candy!

39. A good appetite means a healthy tummy!

40. When a human fasts for two days, fat cells begin to feel desperate!

41. Good food improves a human's mood!

42. You know you're normal if you sneak a piece of candy now and then!

43. If you think the world might end tomorrow, you better eat like crazy today!

44. No, no don't pierce the tongue!

45. I love being a fat cell in his finger because he plays the piano beautifully with my support!

46. Please only one piercing in your ear, we've suffered enough!

47. When one cupcake won't do, have two!

48. If you skip breakfast you will regret it later!

49. Belly laughs are good for the whole body!

50. Singing songs will help you live long!

A Play on Words:
Adjectives/*Fatjectives*

1. Adorable = Fatdorable
2. Positive = Fatositive
3. Splendid = Fatplendid
4. Stylish = Fatylish
5. Popular = Fatopular
6. Exciting = Fatciting
7. Triumphant = Fatriumphant
8. Delicious = Fatlicious
9. Stupendous = Fatupendous
10. Scrumptious = Fatrumptious
11. Powerful = Fatowerful
12. Flavorful = Fatlavorful
13. Fantastic = Fatastic
14. Incredible = Fatcredible
15. Beautiful = Fatutiful
16. Glorious = Fatlorious
17. Luscious = Fatluscious
18. Lovely = Fatovely
19. Gorgeous = Fatorgeous
20. Awesome = Fatesome
21. Superlative = Faterlative
22. Terrific = Faterrific
23. Wonderful = Fatonderful
24. Exceptional = Fatceptional
25. Spectacular = Fatacular
26. Magnificent = Fatnificent
27. Popular = Fatular
28. Glamorous = Fatlamorous
29. Fabulous = Fatabulous

Fatpocrates & Fatistotle

Radial Raconteur

Dueling Divas

Dueling Tenors

Dueling Scales

Fat Cell Depot

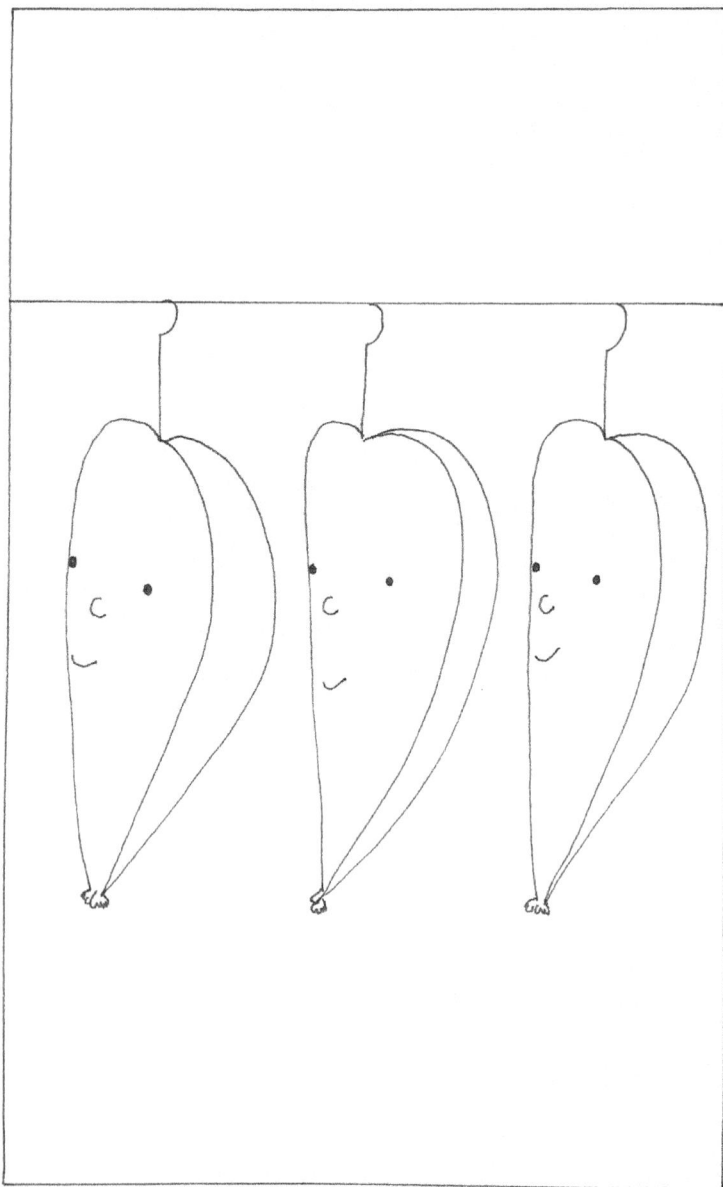

Blockheads

Boneheads

Dunderheads

Fatheads

Four Fat Cells

Guard Cell & Crazy Cell

Guard Cells

Femme <u>Fatales</u>

Dancing Doll

Fat Fellows

Peace Cells

The Fat Cells'
Lilt of Laughter

1. "May there be lots of laughter on your pathway through life."

2. "Arm yourself with some jokes and your defense will be strong."

3. "Laughter demands no payment just a keen ear."

4. "May the sound of laughter bless your ears everyday."

5. "Sometimes when your thoughts need clarity, laughter clears the way."

6. "The heart needs laughter as much as it needs love."

7. "To stifle laughter is to stifle life."

8. "Grow some laughter in your garden of life today."

9. "If laughter were a locale it would be Utopia."

10. "Since no human is an island, share some laughs today."

11. "Laughter is the partner you can always count on."

12. "When your heart feels laughter, it knows relief from woe."

13. "There are no regrets were laughter is concerned."

14. "A chuckle whets the appetite for a hearty laugh."

About the Author

Alice Hutchison is an author, illustrator, and watercolorist. She is a member of the Sierra Club and the National Audubon Society. Her interests include comedy, ornithology, and geology. When Alice isn't writing or creating artwork, she loves to take nature hikes with her husband Alan.

www.ingramcontent.com/pod-product-compliance
Lightning Source LLC
LaVergne TN
LVHW051046080426
835508LV00019B/1737